Coping
WITH
Adversity

Coping
WITH
Adversity

Judaism's Response to Illness and Other Life Struggles

Joel A. Roffman, M.D.
and
Rabbi Gordon A. Fuller

COPING WITH ADVERSITY

© 2008 **Joel A. Roffman, M.D.**
and
Rabbi Gordon A. Fuller

Manufactured in the United States of America

For information, please contact:
Brown Books Publishing Group
16200 North Dallas Parkway, Suite 170
Dallas, Texas 75248
www.brownbooks.com
972-381-0009

A New Era in Publishing™

ISBN-13: 978-1-934812-22-8
ISBN-10: 1-934812-22-6

LCCN: 2008930428

1 2 3 4 5 6 7 8 9 10

DEDICATION

Joel Roffman

I dedicate this book . . .

To my wife, Nancy, who inspired the writing of this book, has filled my life with love and fun, and makes every day worthwhile. Nancy embodies what a wife, a mother, and a daughter should be. I am blessed beyond words that she has chosen to spend her life with me.

To my daughter, Leah, who has brought me more joy, has given me more reasons to be proud, and has bestowed upon me more love than any father could reasonably expect.

To my brother, Mark, who has been a guiding light and a friend to me every day of my life. I look up to him now as I did as a child.

To my patients, who have taught me, challenged me, and inspired me.

In memory of . . .

My dad, who died when I was very young, but whose kindness to others I still remember.

My mom, who personified faith and optimism, and whose boundless love was a source of strength to me in good times and in bad times.

My son, George, who was amazingly resilient in the face of awful adversity. His cheerful countenance in his too-short life still shines on me and on all those whose lives he touched.

Gordon Fuller

To my life partner and best friend, Sharon, whose support and encouragement have been unfailing and whose suggestions are always helpful, you are truly my ezer k'negdi. If the next thirty are half as good as the last thirty, I'll be a very happy (and old) man.

To my children, Evan and Jessica, Eliana and Ben, all of whom are incredible human beings who make me incredibly proud and who will also, I'm sure, pass our wonderful values on to the next generation of Jewish children.

And to all my teachers, counselors, advisors, friends, and mentors, but especially to Rabbi Frank Joseph and to harav Yithak ben Dov Hacohen, mori, achi, y'didi, without whom I would not be the person I am today.

TABLE OF CONTENTS

PART I
COPING WITH ILLNESS & PHYSICAL LIMITATIONS

PART II
COPING WITH OTHER CHALLENGES OF LIVING

PART III
COPING AS WE FACE THE END OF LIFE: OURS AND OTHERS'

PART IV
LESSONS LEARNED

ACKNOWLEDGMENTS

As authors, we are grateful for the opportunity to share this project with each other. The book was a true partnership, and the friendship and respect we share were the keys to its successful completion.

We appreciate Leah Roffman and Dr. Wendy Harpham for their reading of the text and (sometimes) pointed comments and suggestions. We are also grateful for Dr. Harpham's foreword.

We thank Amy Healey, Danny Siegel, Rabbi Judith Abrams, Rabbi Lawrence Kushner, Jackie Waldman, and Arthur Kurzweil for their comments, suggestions, and encouragement.

The staff at Brown Books could not have been more helpful and professional. They were supportive and efficient, and we appreciate them.

We acknowledge with much gratitude permission to include the following:

Excerpt from *Letter in the Scroll* by Simon and Schuster, 2000. Reprinted with permission.

Excerpt from *Does the World Need the Jews?* by Simon and Schuster, 1997. Reprinted with permission.

Excerpt from *Man Is Not Alone*, 1951, and *God in Search of Man*, 1955, by Farrar, Strauss and Giroux. Reprinted with permission.

Excerpt from *Sarah Laughed* by McGraw Hill, 2005. Reprinted with permission.

Excerpt from *Strangers to Ourselves* by Harvard University Press, 2002. Reprinted with permission.

Lyrics from *"Fiddler on the Roof,"* reprinted with permission by MTI Shows.

The discussions of the medical aspects of the people described in this book are not meant to convey specific medical advice. Each person and each medical case is unique. If you, our reader, have symptoms that are in any way unusual or worrisome, please consult your doctor at once.

FOREWORD

My cancer diagnosis launched me on a spiritual journey. That's no surprise since serious illness and other life struggles often do. No matter what your beliefs about God and the universe, when your life plans take a major hit, spiritual questions often arise: Why me? Why this? Why now? And useful answers can't be found through fancy blood tests or sophisticated scans.

Even if you are someone who never asks "Why?" and simply accepts whatever comes your way, difficult times demand that you rustle up some courage and fortitude. You'll need them to adjust to unwanted changes and do what needs to be done to get through to better times.

Whatever your challenge—illness or injury, divorce, unemployment, or the loss of a love, you may find yourself searching for wisdom and inspiration. Nowadays, you don't have to look far.

Go online and google "cancer." Within seconds you're facing a screen full of links to information about all aspects of survivorship. Or open up the yellow pages and look under "Alzheimer's." You'll find names and numbers of organizations that can guide and support your new caregiver role to an aging parent with dementia. The insights and advice from experts and veteran survivors may speed or ease your journey.

So why a book on Judaism's response to illness and other life struggles? Because the wisdom of ancient traditions resonates with modern men and women. After thousands of years, this can mean only one thing: it works.

As stated in the introduction, Judaism is a guide for living. Unlike today's textbooks and faddish three-step methods, Jewish teachings are rich with engaging parables and unforgettable images. The Hebrew Bible offers everyone—Jew and non-Jew, believer and atheist—timeless pearls of healthy perspective on coping with adversity.

These ideas and suggestions gave me direction after my cancer diagnosis in 1990, when I vowed to become a Healthy Survivor: a survivor who gets good care and lives as fully as possible. My having access to the best medical information and practitioners helped. But it wasn't enough for coping with my chronic pain and recurrent cancer, the loss of my medical practice, and a poor long-term prognosis that made it unlikely I'd finish raising my three young children.

That's when age-old Jewish values and commandments energized and comforted me like a grandmother's embrace, firm yet loving. Reading the Book of Job helped me find peace with my losses. Hearing the Talmudic encouragement to "pray as if everything depends on God, but act as if everything depends on me" helped me find a healthy balance between trusting and questioning, and between letting go and taking charge.

I was fortunate: although I'd never been a Jewish scholar, my rabbi and my philosophy-professor husband generously shared applicable stories from the Old Testament and helped me appreciate the underlying lessons as they applied to me.

Today, *Coping With Adversity* serves you Jewish wisdom on a platter. With the combined expertise and compassion of a cardiologist and a rabbi, common difficulties that often lead to doctor visits are juxtaposed with brief analyses of applicable Jewish teachings. In each chapter, Dr. Roffman and Rabbi Fuller highlight essential elements of the Jewish response to the particular problem being discussed. Then they offer suggestions of how to apply the teachings to your personal situation, opening your eyes to opportunities for making things better and feeling happier.

Life is for living. By getting good care and living as fully as possible, you can be a Healthy Survivor of whatever adversity challenges you. If you aren't sure how to proceed or you need a little push, turn the page and tap into the healing power of Jewish wisdom.

Wendy S. Harpham, MD, FACP
Best-selling author, *Happiness in a Storm*
Professional speaker
www.wendyharpham.com

INTRODUCTION

SOURCES OF JEWISH HERITAGE

Tevye, a poor milkman and unlikely protagonist for a Broadway play, is the main character in the beloved musical *Fiddler on the Roof*. The story is set in Tsarist Russia, and despite his difficult life there, Tevye finds reason to celebrate: his daughter has become engaged. At this point in the play, Tevye captures the pathos of life in the featured song, "To Life":

> Life has a way of confusing us,
> Blessing and bruising us;
> Drink *l'chaim*—to life!
> God would like us to be joyful even when our hearts lie panting on the floor,
> How much more can we be joyful when there's really something to be joyful for!
> To life, to life, *l'chaim!*

We are blessed in life, and we are bruised in life, but we must embrace life, for it is all we have. And through it all, God expects us to be joyful. The lyrics of this song fully capture the essence of Judaism.

A Guide for Living

At its core, Judaism is a guide for living. While its literature and teachings address the topic of an afterlife (the "world to come"), it is primarily a religion of the here and now, focusing on the lives we live here on this earth. At Jewish funerals, for example, there is little talk of the deceased "being in a better place" or having a "higher mission." Furthermore, there is no sugar-coating tragedy when tragedies occur. Judaism regards illness, suffering, and grief not as "tests," but rather as causes of legitimate sadness and anguish.

1

Judaism has thus developed and emphasized ways of dealing with hardships of all types that occur in the lives of all of us at one time or another. Its great books go back thousands of years and teach lessons that are timeless and universal in their application. These lessons, as they pertain to illness and other struggles of life, will be the subjects of this book. While the lessons may stem from Jewish tradition, our belief is that anyone, regardless of his or her faith—indeed, regardless of whether or not one even identifies with any religion at all—may be able to learn from these lessons and use them to improve all lives.

This book looks at a number of situations faced specifically by patients in a cardiology practice in metropolitan Dallas, but these cases are all situations that any of us could face at any point in our lives. Some of them required an individual to make very difficult decisions that would greatly impact the life of the patient involved—sometimes the individual's parent, spouse, or child. Some cases involved work or interpersonal relationships such as we all may face from time to time and don't necessarily have medical implications. As I reflected on my medical practice, I realized that much of it entailed counseling patients, sometimes as important as treating specific diseases. My Jewish values guided and assisted me in helping these patients regardless of their religion and regardless of the strength of their faith. My experience with a number of them formed the basis of this book.

The Jewish religious heritage draws on traditions and teachings that span 3,700 years. It gives us access to an incredible wealth of information, experience, and values that can help and guide us in our decision making. Over the millennia and in many different locations, some Jewish traditions have changed and adapted as their people have faced different challenges. Still, there are consistent values that have continuously served those who look to them for guidance and wisdom.

The lessons of Judaism apply to virtually any of life's crises that befall us. They provide a framework, helping to steer our behavior and our approach to issues in early life as well as in older age. The teachings direct our lives toward things that really matter, so that our lives will matter. They serve as a guide—blueprints for action. To a large extent, in Judaism you are what you do.

Moral Authority of the Bible

Why are the adages, lessons, and commandments of Judaism more than mere suggestions—why are they authoritative to Jews, even those who do not necessarily believe that the Bible is the actual "spoken" word of God? The answer goes back to the wisdom of the Jewish tradition gathered over thousands of years. This wisdom, now taken for granted by so many, includes precepts and laws that were revolutionary in their day, yet they had staying power and have earned acceptance by people of all faiths. Indeed, the concepts form the foundation of our own constitution.

Included are the admonitions to treat all people as equals and to sanctify life—all lives, to shun evil and do good (Psalms 34:15), to pursue justice (Deuteronomy 16:20), and to seek peace rather than war (Isaiah 2:4). These concepts and instructions were new at the time and were quite different from the way people and communities had behaved. The love of one's neighbor and the avoidance of gossip and hurtful speech (Leviticus 19:15–18), the importance of the family structure (Leviticus, Ch. 18; Talmud Yevamot 62b), and many more such ideas (Leviticus, Ch. 18, 19) had never before been taught.

Such was the brilliance and moral authority of these concepts that had they come in the form of advice from a wise old relative, any other piece of advice from that relative would most certainly be considered seriously. This hypothetical relative—so wise and advanced in thought—would merit serious consideration and even obedience when giving advice on a whole host of topics.

The teaching of these values begins in the Hebrew Bible, known in most Western countries as the Old Testament. The term for this collection in the modern Hebrew language is *TaNaKh*, which is actually an acronym for its three components: *Torah, Nevi'im*, and *Ketuvim*. We will be referring to these works throughout the book, and a brief description is thus in order here.

The Torah, the Prophets, and the Writings

The word "Torah" comes from a word that means "instruction" or "enlightenment." The Torah is made up of the five books of Moses: Genesis, Exodus, Leviticus, Numbers, and Deuteronomy. It contains the 613 commandments that Jews believe God has given them, instructing them as to how to conduct themselves during their lifetimes. Its stories include the creation of the world (Adam and Eve), Cain and Abel, Noah and the flood, the Tower of Babel, the patriarchal families (Abraham, Isaac, and Jacob), and the Exodus from Egypt, which covers the forty years of wandering to the border of the Promised Land.

"Nevi'im" refers to the books of the prophets and includes the so-called major prophets: Joshua, Judges, Samuel I, Samuel II, Kings I, Kings II, Isaiah, Jeremiah, and Ezekiel. Also included are the twelve minor prophets: Hosea, Joel, Amos, Obadiah, Jonah, Micah, Nahum, Habakkuk, Zephaniah, Haggai, Zechariah, and Malachi.

"Ketuvim" means "writings" and includes the following books: Psalms, Proverbs, Job, Song of Songs, Ruth, Lamentations, Ecclesiastes, Esther, Daniel, Ezra, Nehemiah, and Chronicles I and II.

The Torah is referred to as the "Written Law." It is also the "Constitution" of the Jewish people. However, there is one important difference between this text and the constitution of the United States: there is no legislative option for writing new laws and very little executive power for enforcing the laws. They are basically between God and the individual.

The Talmud

There is, however, an interpretive possibility that rabbis began to employ when they first began to teach the laws after the destruction of the First Temple in Jerusalem in 586 B.C.E. (Before the Common Era). These interpretations eventually became known as the "Oral Law," which was codified in approximately the fourth or fifth century of the Common Era (C.E.) and became known as the *Talmud*. In addition to interpretations and explanations of the Written Law, it also provides some laws to "fill in the gaps."

For instance, most people are familiar with the commandment in the book of Exodus to "Remember the Sabbath day and keep it holy." While we understand that this commandment comes *mi'd'oraita* (from the Torah), it is too vague to be instructive on its own. How is this law to be followed? What types of activities are permitted on the Sabbath? Which are forbidden? The laws that fill in the gaps or are interpretive are called *mi'd'rabbana*n (from the rabbis). Many such laws are found in the Talmud and, in the case of Sabbath, include instructions to avoid engaging in commerce and to refrain from writing (thereby "creating").

Finally, the Talmud itself is comprised of two parts. The *Mishnah*, which is in Hebrew, contains those rabbinic laws that the rabbis at the time agreed were the necessary interpretations and explanations. The *Gemara*, which is primarily in Aramaic, is an interesting compilation of the discussions and concerns that were raised in deciding on the rabbinic laws, as well as some elucidating stories.

In the case studies contained in this book, issues will be presented that affect many of us at various times in our lives. There will be a discussion of how Jewish values inform our reactions and responses to the various problems addressed. Wherever possible, specific sources will be cited for those who would like to study further. Where appropriate, medical references are also included.

The biblical texts cited show that while prayer certainly plays a central role in the ritual lives of observant Jews, it is important to realize Judaism is not a religion strictly about belief or about faith. Rather, it is a religion that places far more emphasis on deeds and behavior. This is why it is focused on the here and now, rather than on some future unknown afterlife. It follows then that although there are many commandments and rituals within the faith, the emphasis is on action. Thus, when the Egyptians chase after the Jews in the story of the Exodus, God admonishes the Jews for praying, saying to Moses, "Why do you cry out to me? Tell the Israelites to go forward" (Exodus 14:15). In other words, there is a time for prayer and a time for action. We will see how this concept applies to one of the cases in a later chapter.

Four Principles and Values

Judaism emphasizes that there are overarching values and principles with respect to how we view life and how we treat people. Four of these values will appear time and again in a number of the case studies and warrant some discussion in this introduction.

The first and foremost principle concerns how we treat others. The Bible states that human beings are created by God in the Divine Image (Genesis 1:26, 27). Therefore, each of us has some degree of innate divinity that warrants our being treated with dignity. Having been created in the image of God, we are obliged to treat each other with great care, avoiding the desecration or abuse of the body and the soul. This concept of innate divinity is the basis for how people are expected to treat other people.

The second principle involves the gift and value of life itself and teaches us how we should care for ourselves. Jews see life as a gift from God that must be protected at all costs. This principle is the basis for the Jewish belief that our bodies and our lives are not just our own, given to us to do whatever we please with them. Rather, the Talmud points out that since all human beings came from one man, Adam, the destruction of one life is tantamount to destroying the entire world. Similarly, the saving of one life is equivalent to saving the entire world (Mishnah Sanhedrin 4:3). We also deduce that since we are all descended from the same ancestors, no one is inherently more valuable than another by means of his or her family, education, or wealth. We are all of infinite worth.

The third principle derives from the first two. Judaism is a religion that emphasizes improvement in the quality of life. The purpose of virtually everything Jews are commanded to do is to make life better for ourselves as well as for our families and those around us. The concept of social responsibility and the creation of a just and compassionate society originated in Jewish scripture and is an everlasting strong and common thread in the Jewish community.

These three principles show that there is much in Judaism that teaches us and instructs us how to become more holy, fulfilling our mission to be, as the Bible commands, "a nation of priests and a holy people" (Exodus 19:5–6). Since this book is not about Judaism as a religion, we will limit our discussion to how Jewish teachings and philosophy can help everyone in coping with some of life's specific challenges

The final principle is that although actions, proper and holy actions, are the hallmark of Judaism, Jews are taught to take nothing for granted and to give thanks for the many blessings that are bestowed upon them. For instance, Jews are taught to say special blessings before and after eating. In fact, there are several different blessings before one eats, depending on the type of food that is to be consumed. There are also prayers that one recites upon such diverse experiences as seeing a rainbow, relieving oneself of bodily waste, going to sleep, and awakening. Prayers exist for sad as well as happy occasions, and there is even a prayer to be uttered upon seeing one who is disabled.

Prayers

The multitude of blessings force observant Jews to call attention to things we would otherwise take for granted. They let us know that every moment is precious and sanctify the ordinary by saying words that help us recognize God's role in everything we do and see.

The daily prayers and rituals of Judaism address concerns that we deal with on a day-to-day basis and include numerous references to illness and healing. The central portion of every prayer service in Judaism is called the *Amidah* (literally, "standing," because of the reverence to God that is demonstrated). It is a series of prayers and blessings repeated several times each day, once in each prayer service. Its basic form is over two thousand years old and contains phrases from biblical sources, as well as prayers reflecting our most basic needs and beliefs. Included is a prayer for health and healing:

> *Heal us, O God, and we shall be healed,*
> *Save us and we shall be saved,*
> *The One we praise is you.*
> *Bring healing that is complete for all our illnesses*
> *For you are the faithful and merciful physician.*

Blessed are you, O God, who heals the sick among His people Israel (Jeremiah 17:14).

Since the Biblical period, everyday prayers in Judaism have expressed a concern for those who are ill. In many congregations, it is customary to include a special prayer for the sick and infirm. In our congregations, this prayer is recited during the Torah service. Every member of the congregation has an opportunity to recite the names of those who are ill. The rabbi then recites the *Mi She'beirakh* prayer:

> *May God who blessed our ancestors bless (name) who is ill. May the Holy One, blessed be He, be filled with mercy for him/her, to heal and cure him/her, to strengthen him/her to perfect health, and to speedily send him/her a complete recovery, both in spirit and in body, and let us say, Amen.*

Rabbi Moshe ben Maimon, better known as Maimonides, was a twelfth century Spanish Jew who continues to be regarded as one of the premier philosophers in all of Judaism. He was also a physician, and his writings are regarded by many as illuminating and inspiring. His systematic code of Jewish law is called the *Mishneh* Torah (or "second" Torah because Maimonides understood that his interpretation of the Torah was not as authoritative as the original). It was his way of taking the original teachings of both the written Torah (Hebrew Bible) and the Oral Torah (the Talmud) and condensing them into what he believed to be a more easily understood and accessible form.

Much specific medical advice is given in this work. Surprisingly, some of the advice is still quite relevant. For instance, Maimonides writes that, "Whoever sits idle and does not tire himself . . . even if he eats good foods and keeps medical rules, shall have pains all his days and his strength shall weaken.

Many of the ills which overtake man are due either to eating bad food or because he fills himself grossly full" (Treatise 2, Ch. 4, Sect. 14).

The main purpose of Maimonides's health rules as stated in the Mishneh Torah, however, was to advise Jews how to serve God properly. "It follows that a healthy and sound body is in the Lord's path, for it is impossible to understand or grasp knowledge of the Creator if one is sick" (Treatise 2, Ch. 4, Sect. 1).

In Psalm 41, we read of God's protection of any who visit those who are ill or are in distress:

> *Happy is he who is thoughtful of the wretched;*
> *In bad times may the Lord keep him from harm.*
> *May the lord guard him and preserve him;*
> *And may he be thought happy in the land.*
> *Do not subject him to the will of his enemies.*
> *The Lord will sustain him on his sickbed.*

This idea is reinforced in the Talmud, where in addition to Jews' responsibility to properly care for themselves, we read that it is considered a good deed to visit those who are ill and infirm (Shabbat 127a). Included elsewhere in this work are specific rules governing how, when, and when not to visit the sick (Nedarim 39a–41b).

An Explanation of the References

As mentioned, the Hebrew Bible is divided into three sections: the Torah, the Prophets, and the Writings. Biblical references provide the name of the book with the chapter and verse. For example, "Genesis 4:21" corresponds to the twenty-first verse of the fourth chapter of the book of Genesis.

Additionally, there are books of *Midrash* (explanations) on a number of books of the Hebrew Bible. These are homilies written during the first Millennium C.E. that elucidate particular verses or stories in some of the biblical books. These citations follow the Biblical reference model above. For instance, "Genesis Rabbah 10:20" references a *midrash* on the twentieth verse in the tenth chapter of Genesis.

The Talmud is comprised of six "Orders," or categories: *Zera'im* (seeds), *Moed* (festivals), *Nashim* (women), *Nezikin* (damages), *Kodashim* (holy things), and *Tahorot* (ritual purity issues). Within each order are a number of Masechtot or sub-classifications (tractates) of the Orders. The most well known of these tractates is Avot, in the Order Nezikin. It is also called *Pirkei Avot* (Ethics of the Fathers).

Talmudic references typically give the name of the tractate, the chapter, and the number of the explanation. If a Mishnah is being cited, the reference appears as "Mishnah" with the tractate name, the number of the chapter, and the number of the Mishnah. For instance, "Mishnah Sanhedrin 4:3" identifies the third Mishnah in the fourth chapter of the Tractate Sanhedrin. The letters "a" and "b" appear in references from the Gemara, designating the side of the page on which the reference appears.

The Intent of This Book

Who among us doesn't feel that we have faced significant adversity in our lives? Overwhelmed with class assignments, my college classmate Ethan lamented his difficulties to our organic chemistry professor, Dr. John Lorand. "Life is hard," Ethan moaned. Probably surprised to hear such an utterance from a nineteen-year-old, Dr. Lorand replied, "Compared to what?" Dr. Lorand's message was that difficulties are simply part of living, for college students as well as for everyone else.

As we will see, Judaism has much to say about many of these difficulties. We will discuss issues of aging, illness, finances, and work. We will also discuss how Judaism teaches us to interact with others, care for our bodies, and make the world a better place. The intent of this book is not to try to convert anyone to Judaism or its way of thinking. Rather, we simply strive to show, from a cardiologist's experience and from a rabbi's perspective, how this religion's ancient teachings and wisdom can help all of us cope with hardships—both the expected and the unplanned.

As you read through these case studies and see how the Jewish tradition can speak to the issues and challenges that are presented, we hope you will gain some understanding of that tradition. Hopefully, you will find parts of it helpful in the challenges you are facing or may face in the future.

PART
ONE

COPING WITH ILLNESS
& PHYSICAL LIMITATIONS

CHAPTER 1

<hr>

COPING WITH THE INEVITABLE WEARING DOWN OF THE BODY

Betty's Case: *"I used to be a dancer."*

Betty sat in my office with her walker, an oxygen tank at her side. "Look at me now," she said. "I used to be a dancer."

Indeed, she had been more than just a dancer. Betty had moved to Dallas after high school from rural East Texas to join a dance company. She danced professionally for a couple of years, mostly in modern dance. Ballet, however, was her passion. After her career was over, she raised a family and began her own ballet company. The company grew, and through this business, Betty introduced generations of young children to the lovely art of ballet.

During Betty's era, women were not usually entrepreneurs, but Betty was an unusual woman. She had been unconventional in her early days, having moved away from her family when that was quite uncommon and considered bold. Beginning her own company was simply an extension of Betty's drive and personality.

Medical Diagnosis

I had known Betty for sixteen years, since she was sixty-five years old. She first presented to my office because of shortness of breath. At that point, tests showed that Betty had a weak heart muscle, a condition known generically in cardiology as a cardiomyopathy. Weakness of the heart muscle can be due to a number of causes. In Betty's case, poorly treated high blood pressure had caused her heart to gradually weaken, and a diet very high in salt caused fluid retention. The weak heart muscle and the high-salt diet conspired to cause fluid to build up in her lungs, and thus she became short of breath. At the time, the condition was relatively easy to treat. Once we diagnosed her problem, Betty was compliant with her medications, altered her diet, and enjoyed symptomatic improvement for a number of years.

Her shortness of breath recurred a year or so ago, but my evaluation revealed no major change in her cardiac condition. However, her chest x-ray was abnormal at the time, and she was sent to a lung specialist. There, Betty was found to have an unusual condition called pulmonary fibrosis, in which the lungs' connective tissue restricts the motion of the air sacs, resulting in an inability of the lungs to extract oxygen from the air. Shortness of breath is the result. This condition is not curable and is often progressive, though symptoms can usually be managed for a time with medication.

Unfortunately, the medications used to treat this condition are not necessarily gentle on the heart and the rest of the body. As is so often the case in internal medicine, dysfunction of one organ system caused problems in other systems. In Betty's case, the medicine caused her to retain fluid and bruise easily, often, and for no apparent reason. It also caused her to experience weakness in her muscles.

To make matters worse, Betty's bone marrow was a bit sluggish in the manufacture of new blood cells—a condition known as myelodysplasia. With her heart and lung disease, Betty needed all the red blood cells she could muster, but she couldn't produce enough of them to compensate for her other conditions. Her shortness of breath was thus worsened. Betty now required oxygen all the time and was still somewhat short of breath with even minimal activity.

Betty also had what I playfully call "Calendar Disease"— aches and pains that are part of the aging process. Arthritis had caused her walking to become painful and her balance to deteriorate, necessitating the use of a walker.

Betty's Disposition

Still, Betty came to my office using her walker's basket to carry a batch of cookies for the office staff. Betty also carried her trademark good humor. Though pale and stooped in posture, Betty was clearly concerned about her appearance, wearing pretty pearl earrings and a necklace to match. Her daughter, who had helped plan a surprise eightieth birthday party for Betty last year and who helps keep track of Betty's appointments and medications, brought her mother to my office.

Betty has been a widow for ten years, but she is still surrounded by loving family and friends. Her children and grandchildren may be spread across the country, but Betty feels close with them and relates stories to me at every visit about their careers and families. I marvel at Betty's approach to life; each new health issue is a challenge that she is determined to meet. In fact, each interaction is an opportunity to spread cheer and to distribute homemade cookies. She appears in my office with an unfailingly bright smile and always asks about my family.

Betty understands that physical capacity is relative, and therefore she's not about to mope about her condition. She understands and appreciates the fact that she was blessed to enjoy many years of exquisite physical ability. Despite the gradual waning of this ability over the years, Betty still has much to contribute to her family and those with whom she comes into contact.

Is the Glass Half Empty or Half Full?

As another example of this approach, consider professional athletes at the end of their careers. By most standards, they are still incredibly well conditioned, yet relative to their professional standards their athletic ability has declined considerably. In the office, Betty noticed a picture of me on a bicycle, completing a very long bicycle ride to benefit the Multiple Sclerosis Society. My pace is a bit slower than it used to be, but I can still complete the ride. So is the glass half empty or half full? I choose to focus on the positive—that is, I can still finish the ride. And in the future when my ability to ride long distances declines, I hope to still see the glass as half full—I will still be able to ride my bicycle, albeit for shorter distances. And later still, when I'm no longer able to ride at all, just being able to awaken to a day of activities will be the victory that I hope to see myself achieving.

THE JEWISH RESPONSE

Betty personifies a number of teachings in the Jewish tradition. First, Judaism teaches us to receive everyone *b'sever panim yafot* (with a cheerful countenance) (Pirkei Avot 1:15). This gesture, we are told, will ensure that we will enjoy warm camaraderie and will build lasting relationships. Certainly, spreading good cheer is one of Betty's most enduring features.

The Talmud asserts that *mitzvah goreret mitzvah* (performing one commandment leads to the performance of another) and similarly *aveirah goreret aveira* (committing one sin leads to committing another) (Pirkei Avot 4:2). Perhaps this is the Bible's way of saying that it is up to us to focus on the positive. The more we do so—the more good deeds we perform and the more positive interactions we have with others—the more easily we will be able to continue being positive in our outlook on life.

Focusing on the positive begets good cheer and good deeds, and this attitude in turn begets better personal interactions, resulting in better relationships and enjoyable activities about which we can be grateful. In this sense, Betty is a great example of positive feedback.

Many people mistakenly believe that the Hebrew word "mitzvah" frequently mentioned and discussed in Judaism, means "good deed." In fact, it means "commandment," indicating that it is one of the things God wants us to do. We learn the specifics of these commandments explicitly from the Torah and implicitly from the Talmud. We also learn them from later rabbinic law. Many of these commandments, such as adhering to the dietary laws of Judaism or properly observing the Sabbath, involve only the individual involved. Many of the commandments, however, particularly those that instruct us how to behave toward our fellow human beings, involve acts that would in fact be considered good deeds, such as taking care of the poor, orphans, and others in need of help. Also included are such altruistic acts as visiting the sick, accompanying the dead to their final rest, being hospitable, and welcoming strangers.

Although she is not Jewish, Betty clearly embodies the spirit and intent of many of these mitzvot. Her gesture of bringing baskets of cookies to people with whom she interacts is her way of being hospitable. By exhibiting cheerfulness and her characteristic good humor, Betty certainly fulfills many of God's commandments, even though her life is difficult and uncomfortable in many ways.

Overcoming Physical Infirmities

Throughout the patriarchal and matriarchal stories in the Torah, we find very imperfect, flawed human beings. None of them was perfect, yet they are still our moral and ethical "superheroes." Many even overcame physical infirmities. For example, Moses, the greatest leader the Jews ever knew and the spokesperson for the entire people of Israel, had an unspecified type of speech impediment (Exodus 4:10). When faced with God at the burning bush, he used that physical flaw as an excuse for why he should not be chosen for such an important leadership role. Yet as we know, God was persuasive, and the entire fifth book of the Torah, Deuteronomy, consists primarily of Moses's orations.

Physical infirmity also afflicted Jacob, another of Judaism's patriarchs. After his encounter with a mysterious being (some scholars argue that he may have been struggling with God) the night before he confronted his long lost brother Esau, he emerged victorious, but would henceforth walk with a limp (Genesis 32:25–33). That night, he was also blessed with the new name of Israel, which literally means "one who wrestles with God." The Jews have been known as b'nai yisrael (the children of Israel) ever since. Though Jacob was never physically the same after that nocturnal encounter, he continued with his mission in life, and he was eventually reunited with his favored son, Joseph. Before he died, Jacob was also fortunate to have the opportunity to bless his grandchildren.

Soul and Body

Judaism teaches that the body is deserving of respect and care, but the neshamah (the soul) is a separate entity. Specifically, the body is the mechanical vessel that carries around the soul (Leviticus Rabbah 34:3). While this vessel might deteriorate with time and with illness, the soul remains, and according to some Jewish teachings, lives on after the death of the body. The implication, of course, is that the worth of an individual is not determined by the physical health of the body, but, to quote Dr. Martin Luther King, Jr., "by the content of the character." Judaism also teaches us to respect the elderly: "You shall rise before the aged and show deference to the old (Leviticus 19:32)."

Of course, no one knows how long Betty will be able to continue, given her limited activities, but she clearly is a woman who knows how to make each moment count. She is able to face each day with a pleasant countenance and a positive attitude. This attitude has given her the strength to continue her life to this point, despite the various health hurdles in her path.

One may look at Betty and sympathize with her because she has so many infirmities, and because, in the physical sense, her future offers little reason for optimism. But that would be the wrong way to view Betty's situation and even her life. Instead of possibilities, Betty has realities that she has already achieved, she has fulfilled many of her dreams, she has performed countless good deeds, and she has cultivated meaningful relationships with her family and friends. Best of all, Betty isn't through yet.

I recall watching Jack Chase, a television newscaster in Boston in the late 1950s and 1960s, who ended his newscasts by saying, "So long . . . and make it a good day." Now decades later, my memory still provides me the sight and deep baritone sound of the balding Jack Chase. (The memories, like the televised pictures at the time, are in black and white.) What struck me even as a child was Mr. Chase's premise that it was up to us to make it a good day. We weren't totally dependent on outside forces to determine whether our day would be a good one. How empowering!

Importance of Our Frame of Reference

A man referred to as *The Ba'al Shem Tov* (owner of the good name) is often credited with being the founder of the Hassidic movement. This is a movement within Judaism that is several centuries old and incorporates mystical beliefs into traditional Judaism. One of the many stories about him describes what happened when he faced death. He was granted anything he wanted for his last wish. Being the great man and rabbi that he was, rather than thinking of anything for himself or his family, he asked to be shown the difference between the *Olam Haba* (literally, the world to come—heaven) and *Gehinnom* (hell). His wish was immediately granted.

The Angel of Death appeared and wordlessly beckoned him to follow. The Ba'al Shem Tov did so and soon entered an elevator. The doors closed and the elevator began to descend. He presumed that he was on his way to Hell. On the trip down, the Ba'al Shem Tov began fantasizing about what this horrible place might be like, replete with all the fiery and unpleasant images he had learned about.

His eyes were closed in anticipation of these horrible visions when the elevator stopped and the door opened. But to his surprise, when he opened his eyes, the scene was one of much pastoral beauty. There were gently rolling hills with beautiful trees, shrubs, and flowers everywhere. There was also a winding path leading from the elevator to a castle off in the distance. He couldn't believe the incredible beauty of what was in front of him! He turned to ask the Angel of Death to explain, but he saw that he was being beckoned simply to follow him down the path.

As they got closer, he beheld the beauty of the castle. Eventually, the two arrived at the doors which opened, allowing the Ba'al Shem Tov to hear faint sounds coming from within. The hallway they entered had incredible tapestries and luxurious carpeting. This led to a room at the end of the hall. As the doors of the room opened, he could now tell that the sounds he had heard were coming from inside—sounds that seemed very unpleasant.

When they finally got to the room, he was again surprised. Before them lay the biggest table he had ever seen, laden with appetizing food and drink. People were sitting in front of this incredible smorgasbord, but now he clearly heard that the sounds were cries of agony and frustration, for he saw that the people sitting around the table had their arms bound from their shoulders to their hands, so that they were unable to maneuver any of the fantastic food and drink into their mouths. The Ba'al Shem Tov, too, started weeping at the sadness he saw in front of him. He realized this scene was the hell he had asked to see, and he was soon back in the elevator with the Angel of Death.

The elevator began to ascend and thus began the journey to what the Ba'al Shem Tov assumed would be heaven. He couldn't get the sounds and images of what he had just witnessed out of his mind, when the elevator stopped and its doors again opened. Surprisingly, before the Ba'al Shem was the exact same pastoral scene as the one he had witnessed in hell—the same gently rolling hills with the trees, shrubs, and flowers, the same beautiful spring-like day, and the same winding path to the castle in the distance.

He looked at the Angel of Death and began to ask what all of this meant, but was again beckoned to follow the path. Arriving at the castle he saw the same carved wooden doors, the same beautiful tapestries and carpeting, and the same room at the end of the long corridor. As they approached the room, the doors opened, and he heard the sounds coming from inside—only this time, they were sounds of joy and merriment.

When he finally got to look inside, he saw the same tables beautifully decorated and again laden with festive food and drink. And when he looked at the people enjoying this feast, he saw that their arms were also bound from the shoulder to the hand. But here, in this room, each one had learned to pick up the food and feed it to the person next to him, so each one was able to enjoy and be satisfied.

The moral of the story is clear: it is up to us to make heaven or hell by the way we live our lives. If we live each moment of our lives in service to others, appreciating what we have rather than focusing our attention on what we lack, we will find heaven right here on earth.

Betty's Gratitude

Betty is not one to wallow in self-pity. She understands that no one has a monopoly on sorrow and hardship. Our entire population of older citizens would fit into a convention hall if it consisted only of those who have never faced hardship in their lives.

Yes, Betty needs a walker, but she's still able to function and enjoy time with her family. Without the walker, Betty might fall and break her hip, causing her to be bedridden for a lengthy time. She is thus grateful for the walker. Without the availability of portable oxygen, she would be constantly short of breath, so Betty is thankful for the oxygen as well. She is certainly grateful that she has a caring daughter who is able to bring her to the office for her appointment, and she is even grateful for my pleasant and caring nurse, Gayle, to whom she gives her homemade cookies. Finally, she is thankful that she still has her full mental faculties. Indeed, Betty awakens each day determined to "make it a good day."

Life and time change us. As we age, all of us can wistfully look back at things we were once able to do. But Judaism teaches us to live our lives so that when we look back, we can be fulfilled and proud. It teaches us that each moment is precious—we must make the most of our days, "count our blessings," and focus on what we are able to do rather than on our lost abilities.

Making the Most of What We Have

Another Hassidic story tells of Rabbi Zusye of Hanipol, a teacher beloved by his students, who was quite ill and found himself faced with his final moments on earth. He began weeping uncontrollably, and his students quickly gathered near to comfort him. "Are you crying because you are afraid, Reb Zusye? Are you worried that God will ask you why you weren't more like Moses?" they asked. "I am afraid," Reb Zusye replied, "that when I meet my Maker, He will not ask me, 'Zusye, why weren't you more like Moses?' but that he will ask me Zusye, why were you not more like Zusye?'" Are we making the most of our time here on earth? Are we being all we can be?

Is Betty's life diminished by her age and infirmities? Only her physical capacity is weakened. She is still to be cherished as an example of how to deal with our inevitable physical decline. People like Betty are a source of inspiration for all of us by spreading good cheer, being grateful for life's blessings, refusing to let physical limitations define who they are, and trying to make each day a good day. This should be the example toward which we all strive.

APPLYING JEWISH TEACHING

Performing good deeds and spreading cheerfulness results in cheerfulness and acts of kindness being returned to you. A pleasant demeanor encourages people to be pleasant in return. Focusing on the positive in your life results in a positive spiral in which you will find that there is more to be happy about.

While there is much undeniable sorrow that befalls each of us, a large part of what makes for a "good day" as opposed to a "bad day" depends on you. You can help determine for yourself whether your life is more like heaven or more like hell. Much is determined by your own viewpoint and, of course, by your own actions.

Each moment is precious and passes very quickly. Are you doing all you can to appreciate your blessings and to make your days pleasant?

Chapter 2

❦

DEALING WITH LIFE'S ILLNESSES AND HARDSHIPS

Shelley's Case: *"Why did this happen to me?"*

Shelley was in the office for the first time after her recent hospitalization. She had been in the hospital ten days earlier with chest pain. The pattern of her pain, her electrocardiogram, and her laboratory studies made it clear that the pain was from the heart—she was having an "acute coronary syndrome." Essentially, this means that she suffered a stoppage of blood in the coronary arteries, causing pain; if it is not aggressively treated, significant heart muscle damage may result.

Symptoms and Treatment

The Emergency Department personnel had wheeled Shelley immediately to the heart catheterization lab, where a dye test, called a coronary arteriogram, showed blockages in two of the three main arteries that supply the heart with blood. These were successfully opened with stents, metal scaffolding devices that prop open the arteries at the point of maximum blockage.

Her chest pain resolved quickly. Shelley's heart had incurred only a small amount of damage, and she made an uneventful recovery in the hospital. The blockages that caused Shelley's pain are caused by hardening of the arteries. While the most severe blockages were opened, there were other, less severe areas that might ultimately cause the same symptoms and place Shelley in the same danger of a heart attack. With aggressive treatment, we can hope to battle this process to a standstill. Occasionally though, we can only slow the process, which still marches on inexorably.

The Burden of Multiple Medical Problems

Shelley had not anticipated her life evolving this way. She had been a healthy child and young adult, with exemplary health habits. Good health, however, is the result of three factors: good health habits, good genes, and good luck. Unfortunately, Shelley was deficient in the third factor. In her late teens, she was diagnosed with type 1 diabetes. Most often, diabetes occurs later in life and usually in patients who are overweight. We've all heard about the obesity epidemic in our country. One consequence of this is termed "type 2" diabetes. Less common is "type 1" diabetes, which occurs in young people regardless of their weight. Its cause is entirely different, stemming from an immune process that attacks the pancreas and limits insulin production. This disease mandates life-long insulin therapy.

Though Shelley managed her disease well by eating properly and giving herself insulin injections, she now suffered from one of the complications of diabetes—hardening of the arteries. Shelley's diabetes had also caused her to have cataracts. Still another of diabetes's complications is kidney disease, and Shelley had fallen victim to this problem as well. Her internist was monitoring her gradually declining kidney function closely and had recently informed Shelley that a kidney transplant or dialysis might eventually be necessary.

The relatively easy part of Shelley's case was her cardiac problem. The stenting procedure and subsequent medical therapy were straightforward. The far more difficult part was answering her question, "Why did this happen to me?" She was doing her best to be a good daughter, parent, and wife, but at age 49, she found herself increasingly burdened by serious health issues. She was now taking medicine for her heart, her kidneys, and her diabetes and had frequent appointments with a variety of doctors.

Placing Illness in Its Proper Context

Were it not for her medical conditions, Shelley's life would have been satisfying and free of major stressful issues. She had three children who brought her much joy, a son's wedding to look forward to, a loving husband, and a job as a piano teacher that she still enjoyed. Though stoic in the hospital, Shelley began to show inevitable signs of emotionally breaking down. In the office, she appeared worried and angry, expressing frustration to me as she looked for the answer to the question that haunts so many of us: "Why?"

From both a spiritual standpoint and a medical perspective, it is important to lift Shelley out of her emotional abyss. Recent studies show that faith and a healthy mental outlook can be important aspects of healing. In the cardiology literature, a number of recent papers involving patients with heart disease demonstrate a correlation between depressive symptoms and an unfavorable prognosis (Rozanski, A., et al., *Journal of the American College of Cardiology* 45[2004]:637; Sherwood, A., et al., *Journal of the American College of Cardiology* 46 [2005]:656). These studies indicate that what one believes, and therefore what one expects, can have a strong influence over the speed and extent of one's recovery from illness. Focusing on the illness and on all the negative aspects of it can have harmful consequences and impede healing. Conversely, focusing on positive things and envisioning a return to health can be a strong aid in the healing process.

It is thus vitally important to improve Shelley's emotional state. So before we even begin to address her question of "why?" we must try to give her a framework for approaching her illnesses. Shelley needs to cope with her conditions by placing them in the proper context with respect to the rest of her life. One way for her to do this is to attempt to "compartmentalize" her ailments. Certainly, we all must do what is necessary in order to stay as healthy as possible. Beyond that, though, we must put our illnesses into their own mental compartments, tending to them as the need arises, but not letting them dominate our thoughts and thus interfere with the things we enjoy in life.

In light of this, I encouraged Shelley to be positive and to understand that diabetes is not "who she is." It does not define her. She is a mother, a wife, and a piano teacher with many devoted students who depend on her—and hopefully, a future grandparent. These are the things on which she should focus in the course of the day. Shelley's health would be well served by her keeping her mind on the positive and dealing with her medical conditions as necessary, but refusing to let those conditions be the primary factors that characterize her.

THE JEWISH RESPONSE

I am often reminded of a story involving Miriam in the Torah (Exodus 15:20). The Israelites were freed from bondage in Egypt, but having had a change of heart, Pharaoh sent his soldiers after them in the desert. We are all familiar with the story of the parting of the Red Sea (or more accurately in a biblical context, the Sea of Reeds), allowing the Israelites to cross. The sea then returned to its normal state, swallowing the Egyptian army and causing the soldiers to drown. Realizing that they were safe and forever free from Egyptian bondage, the Israelites celebrated in the desert.

We read that Miriam then took out a tambourine and led her people in song and celebratory dance. So while the Israelites, in their haste to leave Egypt, didn't even have enough time to let their bread rise in the ovens, Miriam managed to pack her tambourine! Somehow, she had the optimism to think that although things seemed grim and uncertain, there would, at some point, be reason to celebrate. What a wonderful example for all of us who face medical issues or other trials and tribulations. Looking down the road in anticipation of celebratory events large or small may or may not help in the treatment of various medical conditions, but pleasant thoughts surely make the day more pleasant than it would be by focusing on illness.

Although she didn't appear to blame herself for the conditions that had befallen her, Shelley still asked why all of this happened. It is a question as old as humanity.

The Dilemma of Belief

For many people of faith, a conundrum exists regarding how we understand God. Three characteristics are typically attributed to God—God is omnipotent, or all powerful; benevolent, or a force for good; and omniscient, or all knowing. However, our finite human minds conceive that only two of the three characteristics can be true at the same time. That is, if God is good and omnipotent, then the amount of suffering in the world would lead us to conclude that God does not know about it. By the same reasoning, if God knows about evil and suffering and is a force for good, then God must necessarily be less than omnipotent. Finally, if God is omnipotent and omniscient, knowing all and doing all, then God must directly cause much of what we perceive as hardship and malevolence. From a theological viewpoint, this predicament is commonly known as the problem of evil.

Those who believe that misfortune is caused directly by God postulate a number of possible reasons for their hardship. Some believe that their adversity is God's retribution for sinful behavior. Some regard it as a test from God, to see if they are worthy of heavenly bliss after their death. Others see their suffering as God's way of inspiring them to set an example to others regarding how to cope with adversity. Still others disclaim the whole notion of suffering as punishment, advocating the idea that we cannot see the "whole picture" and cannot know God's plan. In other words, perhaps what we think of as suffering isn't really suffering at all. One would be able to make sense out of illness and suffering only if one could see God's "big picture." In this model, only in the course of eternal time will God's plan become apparent.

Many believe that since God set the laws of nature in motion, He has had little or nothing to do with events here on earth and in the universe. It will only be "at the end of days" that God will call upon us to account for our deeds and our lives. Only then will our hardships and the world's injustices be reconciled. Undoubtedly, theologians and lay people alike will continue to engage in this discussion. For those wishing a more complete discussion on Judaism's concepts of suffering, consult *Knowing God* by Elliot N. Dorff and *A Living Covenant* by David Hartman.

Why Do We Suffer?

When Shelley came to my office for her appointment, she was in physical and emotional pain. It hardly serves her to go through the intellectual exercise of listing all the possible reasons why she has suffered. Similarly, self-blame will be counterproductive, causing only frustration and guilt.

The question of why events as we see them sometimes make little sense troubled even Moses, who asked God to help him understand. "Pray let me know Your ways that I may know You and continue in Your favor" (Exodus 33:13). The answer from

God was that no, this would not be possible, at least not in this world (Exodus 33:20). Despite a strong belief in God (or perhaps because of that belief) Jews have been taught that "It is not in our power to explain either the tranquility of the wicked or the suffering of the righteous" (Pirkei Avot 4:19).

In later Jewish literature dealing with the issue of suffering, we come to the book of Job. He is described as a righteous and good man, yet he is forced to suffer through the deaths of his children, the loss of his wealth, and a painful skin disease. His friends can only deduce that Job must have sinned terribly to have warranted such suffering. Their explanation, though, is rebuked by God. After many chapters of questioning, challenging, death, speculation, and tears, God appears and gives his response to Job:

> Where were you when I laid the earth's foundations?
> Speak if you have understanding.
> Do you know who fixed its dimensions?
> Did you ever command forth a morning?
> Does the hawk spread its wings by your wisdom?
> Does the eagle soar at your command, building its
> nest on high? (Job, Ch. 38 and 39)

Perhaps surprisingly, Job is satisfied by God's answer:

> See, I am of small worth; what can I answer you?
> I clap my hand to my mouth.
> I have spoken once, and will not reply. (Job 40:5–6)

So in Judaism, we have no specific and universally agreed-upon answer to the question of suffering. Why evil and suffering occur is beyond our comprehension, just as it was beyond Job's. We must simply rise above our setbacks and tragedies and strive to give meaning and relevance to our lives.

How Might Shelley Cope?

However we reconcile the occurrence of events that cause sadness—whatever our personal theology—we are left with a world in which there is distress, affliction, and iniquity. Shelley is confronted with serious medical conditions at a relatively young age. She is angry, frustrated, and confused as a result. Many people find that their faith in God becomes stronger and more helpful when they are faced with difficult health or personal issues. For others, the opposite is true. Prolonged suffering destroys their faith and beliefs. But religion will always be more about faith than about facts. There will be no firm and factual answer to Shelley's question of "Why me?" in her lifetime.

Understandably, Shelley's illnesses have affected her outlook on life. We don't know her personal theology, but rather than become disillusioned and angry, searching for answers that do not and will not exist in any objective way, she needs to direct her energy in a positive way. She must acknowledge that she will not find a satisfactory answer in her lifetime.

How do we help those in need or in poor health? Numerous ways come to mind. For example, one of Judaism's mitzvot (commandments) is to visit those who are sick. We do this because we believe it is imitating God's own behavior, for we read (Genesis 17:25–18:2) that God sent an angel to visit Abraham when he was recovering from his circumcision. We also learn from the Talmud (Nedarim 4:4) that the rabbis believed everyone who visits the sick takes away one sixtieth of the ailment when the visit is concluded. The mathematics is less important than the fact that we can lessen pain and suffering by being a source of concern and comfort.

Though she must deal with medical issues, Shelley is currently managing them well. She may also derive benefit from going to visit others who are ill, either with the same illnesses or with different ones. Seeing herself having a positive impact on others may help improve her mental state. Indeed, relishing her role as piano teacher, enriching the lives of her students will help in a similar way.

As we mentioned in the introduction, Jews also have a tradition of saying a special prayer when the Torah (Five Books of Moses) is read at a prayer service. It is called a *mi shebeirach.* These are actually the first words of the blessing, meaning "May the source of blessings who has blessed . . ." There are actually many different ways of concluding such a blessing, depending on the occasion, but the most common way is directed to the ill and suffering. In most congregations, time is taken to read the names of those congregants who are ill and for service attendees to have the opportunity to add other names to this very public and moving way of praying for recovery. The prayer includes healing of the body and healing of the soul.

Shelley may find comfort in making such a prayer request, whatever her faith. Many people in Shelley's situation find great strength in knowing that others are concerned about them and are expressing those concerns through prayer to a Higher Power.

Choose Life

We read in the book of Deuteronomy a review of many of the precepts of the Torah and an explanation of how following these teachings can lead to a life of value and fulfillment. Then we come to one of the most powerful and empowering phrases in the entire Torah: "I have set before you life and death, blessing and curse. Therefore, choose life" (Deuteronomy 30:19).

This textual citation tells us that the preservation of life is of critical importance. It therefore is a message to us as to how precious life is and how we must strive to do everything possible that is worthwhile with the time—and the situation—that we are given here on earth. Shelley has a wonderful, loving family; she can and should look forward to many happy times with them. She needs to focus on their importance in her life. She may also want to take on new hobbies or projects that can add meaning to her life and help her focus on the positive.

We have previously said that God has given each human being free will. While that doesn't mean that we can control everything that happens to us, we can certainly control how we react to that which we encounter. Victor Frankl was a Holocaust survivor whose book, *Man's Search for Meaning*, has been translated into twenty-four languages, selling millions of copies. His salient message in the book is that although we can't always change what happens to us, we are in control of how we react. Our actions and thoughts are under our exclusive domain. Meaning, relevance, and achievement are possible in spite of suffering and adversity. Frankl quotes the philosopher Friedrich Nietzsche: "He who has a why to live for can bear almost any how."

A Model for Shelley to Follow

We have no good answer to Shelley's question of "Why me?" Her health habits are exemplary, and it is unfortunate that she cannot remove the specific diseases that plague her body. She can, however, choose how to react to the hand that she has been dealt. Hopefully, she will find the strength to live her life with courage, with a caring and cheerful demeanor, and with the determination to make the best of the challenges that life brings her way. Helping her every step of the way will be the enveloping and loving support of friends and family.

We must remind people like Shelley that their illnesses are not their fault, that they must remember the power of positive thinking, and that—like Miriam in the Bible—they should keep their tambourines with them at all times. Certainly they will find themselves in situations that call for a celebration. Joyous moments don't have to be grand events like weddings. They can be in the warm smile of an elder appreciative of a kindness shown. They can be in the exhilaration of a child having played a particular piano piece for the first time. They can be in the loving embrace of a spouse, son, or daughter, grateful for the love given. Shelley has and will continue to have many occasions that call for the use of her tambourine. Play it often, Shelley!

APPLYING JEWISH TEACHING

We must not blame ourselves for illnesses (and events) over which we had no control. These are not divine retribution for some awful sin which we have committed.

Although we may not be able to control fully our health, we can control how we live our lives and what our response to illness and adversity will be.

We must not let our illnesses or other misfortunes define us. We have much to be grateful for and must allow ourselves the enjoyment and appreciation of life's blessings.

Chapter 3

Accepting God's Miraculous Help

Leo's Case: *"No surgery for me, Doc. Whatever is meant to be will be."*

Leo had become short of breath over the past several months. At first, he didn't notice. He began to take the elevator instead of the stairs for even a flight or two. Now, he was acutely aware of his breathlessness and could hardly walk into my office from the parking lot without stopping to catch his breath.

Symptoms

I had been treating Leo for a condition known as aortic stenosis in which the aortic valve in the heart (the valve that functions as the door between the heart and the rest of the body) becomes scarred or deformed. This condition causes a strain on the heart, eventually producing chest discomfort, fainting, or shortness of breath. It is generally a slowly progressive disorder, but, once it causes symptoms, it can be effectively treated only with surgery—the replacement of the valve. Leo's condition was ultimately caused by a combination of the aging process and a congenital (present at birth) structural abnormality of the aortic valve.

Over the course of Leo's seventy years, the valve became encrusted with calcium. This is common in heart valves after decades of wear and tear, especially when they are somewhat deformed to begin with. Its movement thus became increasingly restricted. At this point, there was very little space through which blood could exit the heart's main pumping chamber. The heart was not able to increase its output of blood when Leo engaged in physical activity such as stair climbing. The result in Leo's case was severe shortness of breath with even modest activity.

Surgery to replace the valve, like any heart operation, is potentially dangerous. But in a person in otherwise good health and in whom the heart muscle is strong, the risks are low. Without surgery, the prognosis of aortic stenosis is poor. Once the serious symptoms of aortic stenosis occur, more than half of all patients die within a few years. Leo was now in this high risk group, yet he was very reluctant to undergo surgery.

Refusing Medical Intervention

There are several possible reasons why a patient might decline medical and surgical intervention for a life-threatening problem such as critical aortic stenosis. The first is a deep and abiding faith that whatever happens is God's will and that humans have no right to intervene. This belief is the way Christian Scientists approach these issues; they reject medications and surgery because they believe that asking God to restore health is all they are allowed to do. Our society respects an individual's right to determine whether or not to seek medical care, though this deference to the individual is controversial when it involves the children of those whose religious beliefs prohibit surgery. In Leo's case, he certainly has the right to accept or refuse medical care for religious reasons, or for any reason he chooses.

Still along religious lines, others claim to see their illness as a message from God that their life is coming to an end. They have a strong belief in heaven and will not interfere with what they consider a natural act that is divinely ordained. They may have taken medications for various ailments, but a surgical process that involves opening the chest and stopping the heart is too much of an interruption of the natural order for them to accept. So for some, how much medical intervention is acceptable seems to be a matter of degree; medication is fine but surgery is not. However, many of these same people who would not allow themselves to undergo elective medical or surgical procedures might consent to an appendectomy if, for example, their appendix burst, directly and immediately threatening their lives. Perhaps then, there is an inconsistency—if they would consent to emergency surgery, thereby upsetting the natural order, why not surgery for a dangerously diseased heart valve?

Maybe the answer goes beyond religious conviction for some people. For many, the reluctance to undergo procedures like heart surgery involves simple fear. The patient may be fearful of pain and fearful of a long recovery with its attendant loss of independence. Of course, the ultimate fear is of death from the operation itself. Some other patients may be in denial of their predicament. They hope against all evidence that things are not as bad as the doctor is telling them and that they really don't need an operation at all.

There is thus a spectrum of reasons involved here. For some, fear is the driving influence; for others, religion provides the strongest reason. There may be a degree of inconsistency in taking medications for some conditions or agreeing to emergency surgery for the hypothetical ruptured appendix while declining surgical treatment for a diseased heart valve on religious grounds. This stance may be explained, however, by the fear of pain and the loss of independence stemming from having a major operation. Certainly, these are both rational concerns.

Medical Diagnosis

I had known Leo for a number of years, since he was first referred to me for a heart murmur. Though aortic stenosis was the cause of the heart murmur, it caused no symptoms and didn't merit surgery. Now, however, the situation had changed. During Leo's visit, he admitted to me that he was not only short of breath with modest exertion, he was also experiencing some light-headedness. This is an ominous symptom in cases of aortic stenosis, because it signifies the inability of the heart to pump enough blood to sustain a level of full alertness. Repercussions from this condition may include fainting, with its attendant risk of injury. It may even include sudden death from a disorder of the heart's rhythm.

Leo was a retired welder who had grown up as the youngest of three siblings in a small town in Texas. Though not educated beyond high school, Leo was articulate and had always been self-sufficient. He went to work full-time immediately after high school, and he was proud that he had made a decent living, able to provide well for his wife and two children. He was certainly not about to become a burden to his family. After all, he had always been the one to provide care, not receive it.

The Loss of Independence

From my conversations with Leo and his wife, I suspected that there was a combination of factors at play here. It was apparent to me that there may indeed have been a somewhat fatalistic or perhaps religious outlook influencing him. Leo used such phrases as, "No surgery for me, Doc. Whatever is meant to be will be," and "The Man upstairs will decide what happens." Still, Leo feared the operation itself as well as the loss of independence that the surgery would entail, even though his wife constantly implored him not to worry and reassured him that she'd help him get through it. It thus seemed clear to me that fear was a major reason for his reluctance to have his valve replaced—fear of pain, fear of the unknown, and fear of the loss of control and independence.

Many of us may fear a loss of independence. It often results in a role reversal in which the person who had been the caregiver and provider now needs to be the recipient of care and help. Some people are more comfortable in the former role and not very good at "receiving." On the other hand, those with such fears—in this case, Leo—often don't consider how much more of a burden their premature death might be for surviving family members.

For those who fear the loss of autonomy and the discomfort from surgery, time and reassurance often help convince them of the need to take action. The worsening of the patient's symptoms, of course, also plays a role. But perhaps predictably, for those who base their decisions on religious grounds, the situation can be a bit more complicated. Leo's professed fatalistic outlook was just such an example. This outlook needs to be addressed separately.

THE JEWISH RESPONSE

In Judaism, we learn that there is a time for prayer and a time for action. One of the best known stories in the Bible takes place after the Hebrew slaves are released from Egyptian bondage. They arrive at the Sea of Reeds and discover that the Egyptians, having had a change of heart, are now in full pursuit. Will they be recaptured and forced back into slavery? Will they be killed? Should they attempt to cross the forbidding sea?

Upon hearing the fearful cries of his people, Moses prays to God for help, but God rhetorically asks, "Why do you cry out to Me? Tell the Israelites to go forward" (Exodus 14:15). God then tells Moses to hold out his staff and that, when he does so, the sea will split. The Israelites will then be able to walk through on dry land. But a *midrash* (an explanation or commentary on scriptural text) tells us that there was one brave soul, Nachshon Ben Aminadav, who actually ventured into the water before the sea parted. Only when Nachshon showed faith and continued walking until the water was up to his nose did the sea actually recede to the point where the rest of the Israelites were able to cross. God's message to us in this story seems to be twofold: have faith, but take action.

Have Faith but Also Take Action

We also learn from the creation story in Genesis that God created us and gave us free will, which includes the ability to "master the earthly domain" (Genesis 1:26–28). From a Jewish point of view, these two lessons—taking action rather than relying on divine intervention and God's mandate for humans to use the earthly domain to their benefit—legitimizes human achievement and advancement, including, of course, medicine. In this verse, we are told to make the world better for ourselves and for others, and throughout the Bible we are told to make ourselves better for the benefit of the world.

Another section of Genesis (Genesis 2:7) tells us that God created and gave life to Adam, the first human, by "blowing into his nostrils the breath of life." The Hebrew word for "to breathe" is *linshom*, which shares the same root [n-sh-m] as the word for "soul"—*neshamah*. From this we can surmise that our souls are literally the breath of God within us. Surely, it is then our duty to preserve and protect this sacred gift. Many medical conditions are manifested by shortness of breath, a poignant symbol.

The nature of our specific beliefs about God can also have an effect on our outlook toward both illness and intervention. If one believes that it is God's will that one's life is coming to an end, why must God cause suffering? Does God want humans to suffer with long and painful deaths? Bad things happen in the world, including illness and disease. Some may explain these misfortunes by claiming that they are God's judgment and punishment. But many of us believe in a God that is only good and would not cause such pain or punishment. It is therefore up to us as caregivers and loved ones to minimize and, if possible, eliminate distress.

Certainly, those of us who practice medicine don't look upon ill or hospitalized patients as sinners (as Job's friends did) paying the price for their misdeeds. Healthcare providers don't feel that people who are sick deserve their fate. God doesn't want Leo to be sick, dying from his aortic stenosis. Instead, He wants us to "master our domain" and has given us the tools with which to restore Leo to good health. Healthcare workers try to ameliorate the condition of the sick by using the skills and tools bestowed upon them. The evidence for God's existence is perhaps more apparent in our way of coping with the hand we are dealt than with the cards themselves.

When Having Faith Precludes Action

There is a famous story of a man of faith who lived in an area that was beginning to flood. As the rain continued to pour down, he stood on his porch, and a fire rescue truck came to evacuate him. "No thanks," he said. "God will save me—I have faith." The flood waters rose rapidly. When a National Guard boat came by, urging him to get into the boat before it was too late, he responded, "Don't worry, I know that God will save me; I am a man of faith." Finally, the man climbed to the roof of his house, yet the waters still rose. An army helicopter flew overhead and called out over the loudspeaker for him to grab the rope ladder and climb aboard. The man shouted back, "It's OK—God will save me!" The flood waters overwhelmed him and he drowned. The man was crestfallen when he met his Maker and asked, "God, I had complete faith in you! Why didn't you save me?"

God replied, "Save you? I sent you a rescue truck, a boat, and a helicopter! Why didn't you use any of them?"

God did not forsake this poor man. Given all of the supportive measures that were offered him, it is more accurate to say that the man had failed to find God in his surroundings, in the attempts of others to rescue him. In a similar vein, medicine and caregivers are taught skills and are motivated to help those in need. Are they not the works of God? It is nothing short of miraculous that in small pills there are chemicals that scientists have developed with the power to treat various diseases, kill deadly germs, and relieve pain. It is astonishing and marvelous that there are cameras the size of a small capsule that a patient can swallow, so that previously unavailable visual access to the inside of the human body is possible. Step by step, doctors have developed operations that have now been performed thousands of times—operations that can treat the most dangerous of heart disorders and other ailments. If these aren't signs of the wondrous workings of God, what is?

Faith and action are two sides of the same coin. We must learn to depend on both to fulfill our roles as human beings created in God's image. God wants us to have faith, but that doesn't mean that God wants us to be passive. In his presidential inaugural address, John F. Kennedy challenged and inspired us with his words: "With a good conscience our only sure reward, with history the final judge of our deeds, let us go forth to lead the land we love, asking His blessing and His help, but knowing that here on earth, God's work must truly be our own."

We read in Psalms: "The heavens belong to the Lord, But the earth He gave over to man" (Psalms 115:16). And in the Talmud, the advice given is quite simple: "When injury is likely, one should not rely on a miracle" (Kiddushim 39b).

Faith, Confidence, and a Positive Attitude

Sometimes humans may need a more concrete sign of hope to help hold onto faith and overcome fear. This need is illustrated in the Bible with a tale that is perhaps apocryphal, but nonetheless compelling. When the Israelites were trekking through the wilderness, finally on their way to the Promised Land, the first people to attack them were the Amalekites. During the battle between the two groups, Moses held up his arms. When the people saw this, they were encouraged and repelled the attackers, but when he got tired and lowered his arms, they lost strength, and the attackers gained the upper hand. Finally, Moses's brother Aaron and a man named Hur gave Moses a rock to sit on, and each one held up one of his arms. This action provided the necessary confidence for an Israelite victory (Exodus 17:9–13). Certainly, it might be difficult for us to comprehend why the Israelites derived such confidence from a relatively commonplace gesture. Regardless, we can take away from this story the message that confidence is a necessary ingredient to victory.

While this story may reflect more creative writing than historically accurate facts, surely we must acknowledge that well-trained doctors, nurses, and social workers impart helpful treatment and healing. These caregivers, if given the chance, inspire the confidence that aids in the healing process. Loving family and friends may offer further encouragement and may serve as examples of triumph, having coped with and survived their own tribulations. These are all examples of Godliness in our environment.

Faith, confidence, and a positive attitude are all important in helping us overcome physical as well as mental distress. Medical studies help us understand the importance of these factors in the process of healing. For example, a recent study observed more than five hundred patients for fifteen years, first evaluating their mental state with respect to whether they were optimistic about their future. From a health standpoint, the patients were equivalent at the beginning of the study, but those regarded as optimistic based on a patient questionnaire were approximately half as likely to have a heart-related death over the ensuing period of fifteen years. The conclusion of the study was the following: "Dispositional optimism is a relatively stable trait over fifteen years and shows a graded and inverse association with the risk of cardiovascular death." That is, those who are generally more optimistic had a better chance of recovery than those who were generally more pessimistic (Giltay, E.J. et al., *Archives of Internal Medicine* 166[2006]:431).

Four Angels

People of faith may have an additional reason for being optimistic about their health and their recovery from illness. In some religions, this faith involves the help of angels. Angels in Judaism are different from angels in other religions. First, while they are closer to God in some ways, they have no free will. Generally, they are given one task to carry out for whatever time they appear on earth. The Hebrew word for angel, malach, actually means "messenger." But there are four angels who have different missions and who, according to Jewish tradition, surround us at all times. The Angel Michael, whose name literally means "who is like God," is on our right and symbolizes our closeness to God. Gavriel, meaning "strength of God," is on our left and represents our power and our ability to seek treatment in the face of illness, becoming an active partner with our caregiver.

In front of us is *Uriel*, "light of God," educating us, lighting our path, and showing us the way to proper treatment and recovery.

Finally, behind us is *Raphael*, "healer of God," to aid in our well-being. Granted, this leap of faith is one that is not easily made for many people. Imagine, however, how comforting it would be and the optimism it would generate if one could conceive of always being surrounded by angels, one of whom is a healer!

Whether we serve those who are ill as family, friends, doctors, nurses, or others, we need to remember to use our own Godliness to guide us in understanding what a given patient needs and to act as angels. This resolve may involve being like the angel Michael, providing comfort and compassion; Gavriel, providing confidence and courage in the ability to overcome adversity; Uriel, giving us understanding and insight; or Raphael, helping in the healing and recovery process from either an emotional or a physical upheaval.

If Leo sees himself as being surrounded by "angels," personified by his supporting and loving family and by his caregivers, and if he feels that he can be helped by the miracles of modern medicine that God has inspired and provided, he may be better able to overcome his fears and allow himself to be healed.

APPLYING JEWISH TEACHING

God has endowed us with the mandate to master our earthly domain. It is thus our duty to use the means available to us to preserve and protect the sacred gift of life we have been given.

Understanding the needs and fears of our loved ones and acting on this understanding will aid in the healing process.

There is a time for faith and a time for action. Modern medicine is truly a divine gift. Do not turn away from it. Here on earth, our Creator's work must be our own.

Caregivers are also a divine gift. Gratefully accepting their care is a gift we can give in return.

Chapter 4

Caring for Ourselves and Accepting Treatment for Our Health Conditions

Jack's Case: *"Will I need these pills forever? I hate to take medicine."*

Jack was displeased and abrupt when I met him in his first visit to my office. He was much too busy for this. He was a fifty-three year old man who felt that he was in the prime of life. He had just begun exercising and was following a reasonably regimented schedule. In fact, most of Jack's life was regimented, from work to leisure. That regimen most decidedly should not, in Jack's opinion, include pills for high blood pressure (hypertension).

Even more frustrating for Jack was my assertion that although he could affect his blood pressure by changing his diet and smoking habits and by continuing to exercise regularly, I would still need to prescribe medicine for this condition, at least for a while—and most likely indefinitely. He couldn't count on "fixing it" himself. Jack's blood pressure was not in the "borderline" range where I could perhaps defer treatment and recheck it in a month or two. Jack's blood pressure was high enough to cause real harm quickly, and as we shall see, it had begun doing so already.

Reluctance to Take Medicine

Jack was referred by his family doctor because of abnormalities on his electrocardiogram. His blood pressure was elevated at the time of his visit, and his doctor gave Jack a number of things to try. He had been told to redouble his efforts to exercise regularly, become more vigilant about limiting the salt content of his diet, consume less alcohol, and begin to take blood pressure medication. However, all these attempts to change Jack's behavior were to no avail. Jack had tried a number of dietary supplements on the advice of a friend, hoping to avoid the need for prescription medication, but his return trip to his family doctor showed that his blood pressure hadn't budged.

He reluctantly made an appointment to see me, hoping for a "cure" of his high blood pressure. "Will I need these pills forever?" he asked. "I hate to take medicine." What he hoped to hear was, "Here, take these pills for a week and your condition will be gone." But high blood pressure is different. Years ago, it burst into national prominence with a cover story in *Time* magazine entitled "The Silent Killer." For Jack, this would likely be a chronic, dangerous condition, and it would need to be addressed aggressively.

Why does it happen? What is the actual cause of high blood pressure? Sometimes we can find specific reasons and can definitively fix the problem without the use of chronic medication. But, as I am fond of telling patients, the final textbook of medicine hasn't yet been written. We simply don't have a cure for this condition today. In most cases, we can only hope to control hypertension, averting its complications.

The Medical Problem

The abnormality on Jack's electrocardiogram was caused by an abnormal thickening of the heart muscle. Increasing the work of any muscle causes it to become larger and more bulky. When we think of weightlifters and envision the increased size of their arm and leg muscles, we have an idea of what the heart looks like in hypertension, especially in patients who have had this condition for a long time. The blood vessels in the body are constricted—why, we don't always know for certain—and the work of the heart as it propels blood through the circulation is thus increased, ultimately resulting in a "bulking up" of the heart muscle itself. With other muscles, added bulk means greater strength—again, think of the body builder.

The heart muscle, though, behaves differently, and the added bulk eventually causes it to become weaker rather than stronger. This can result in a condition known as congestive heart failure. Other complications of high blood pressure include stroke (indeed, the most common medical precursor of stroke is high blood pressure) and failure of the kidneys. Jack's increased heart thickness and bulk suggested to me that his high blood pressure reading in the office was not caused simply by the stress of the visit itself—"white coat hypertension"—but was more likely to have been present for a rather lengthy period of time. Naturally, once this structural heart change is evident, or once other organs have been affected by hypertension, definitive treatment becomes more urgent. Jack already was showing some cardiac abnormalities from this condition; we should not delay in instituting treatment.

Though Jack wasn't aware of it, his health habits may have contributed to his high blood pressure. He smoked cigarettes and admitted to a chronic cough—likely the early symptoms of chronic bronchitis and lung disease. Additionally, he drank alcohol rather heavily, with martinis his preferred cocktail. Jack consumed two or three martinis a day, amounting to perhaps three to five ounces of alcohol. Additionally, like most Americans, he used too much salt in his diet. Finally, he was mildly overweight and had been physically inactive until very recently.

Many times, there are no such factors contributing to high blood pressure. An individual might have exemplary health habits and still require medication. In these cases, I tell patients that had they not taken such good care of themselves, they might well have needed the medicine much earlier. Jack had a strong family history of high blood pressure and heart disease, and he was thus predisposed to having this condition. He was clearly on a course that was destined to cause him much illness and disability over time.

Preventing Complications

I explained to Jack that blood pressure medicine was not prescribed to make him feel better. I acknowledged that he felt just fine at that point. Instead, the medicine was intended to prevent the complications of hypertension. In fact, virtually all medicine is "preventative." In the case of high blood pressure, we exercise, try to maintain optimal body weight, and eat properly in order to keep our blood pressure in the normal range, hoping to prevent the need for medication.

Once high blood pressure requires treatment, we take medicine in order to prevent its complications: heart failure, kidney failure, and stroke. Once we suffer a complication, we treat the blood pressure and the complications aggressively in order to sustain life and to maximize its quality, hoping to prevent further problems.

Jack's belief that there was little he could do to lower his blood pressure was incorrect. Medical studies have shown that reducing excessive alcohol consumption and eliminating cigarette smoking might help lower blood pressure (in addition to reducing the risk of lung disease and cancer in the case of the cigarettes and reducing the risk of liver disease, heart disease, and anemia in the case of alcohol). Similarly, eliminating excessive salt in the diet and slimming down toward an ideal body weight may also help lower a person's blood pressure, reducing the amount of medication needed, or in some cases even eliminating the need for it altogether.

So will Jack indeed need these pills "forever," as he feared? "Forever," I told him, "is a long time. Let's just say that you need them for now."

THE JEWISH RESPONSE

What do the Jewish texts say about taking medicine and caring for ourselves? How do these lessons apply to Jack?

The Jewish view is that the body is created by God, and it therefore belongs to God. It is merely loaned to us for our lifetimes. Our responsibility is to take good care of our bodies. Just as taking medicine to preserve one's health is a way of honoring God, abusing one's body can be seen as a way of offending God. The basis for this is the commandment found in the Bible, in which we are told to "guard yourself and guard your body carefully" (Deuteronomy 4:9). There are also other sources that teach us to "sanctify ourselves" (Leviticus 11:44) and to "put the Israelites on guard against their impurity, lest they die through their impurity by defiling My Tabernacle which is among them (i.e., by abusing the body I gave them)" (Leviticus 15:31). This theme is also found in Psalms 139:14:

I praise you,
For I am wholesome, wondrously made;

Your work is wonderful;
I know it very well.

Seek Medical Care When Necessary

In addition to an individual's obligation under Jewish law to care for the body and to take whatever measures may be necessary to insure continued good health, there is also an obligation to seek medical care when necessary. In Exodus 21:19–20, we read that an assailant must take proper measures to provide for the restoration of health to his victim. Joseph Caro, a sixteenth century rabbi, wrote an important and enduring code of Jewish law called the *Shulchan Aruch*, in which he advises us to remove obstacles that constitute a danger to our health. He states, "The Torah gave permission to the physician to heal; moreover, this is a religious precept and is included in the category of saving life, and if the physician withholds his services, it is considered as shedding blood" (Yoreh De'ah 335:1, as quoted in Dorff).

In another midrash, we read of two rabbis who give medical advice to a man. They are admonished for doing so by another person, who reasons that perhaps God willed this man to be ill, and the rabbis have no business in interfering with the divine edict. The rabbis reply that, just as a gardener must plow and care for soil so that it yields its harvest, "So, too, the human body is a tree, a healing potion the compost, and a physician is the tiller of the soil" (as quoted in Bialek, 594–595). Just as we must work the soil to bring forth food, we must sometimes administer medicine to improve health.

Maimonides's Mishneh Torah is an authoritative compilation of Jewish law written by the twelfth century Jewish physician and rabbi. In it, he lists the conditions that a city must meet in order for it to be rendered suitable for habitation. Among other things, Maimonides states that there must be a physician and a surgeon in residence, and there must also be a bath house. For many centuries, healing, good health, and cleanliness have been important to Jews.

Taking Proper Care of the Body; the Limits of Longevity

There are commandments in Judaism prohibiting us from piercing our flesh or tattooing our skin. Historically, this was primarily to avoid what were considered to be pagan practices, tantamount to idol worship. We also now understand that any time one pierces the skin, there is a risk of infection with a number of potentially serious diseases such as hepatitis and AIDS.

Tattooing, piercing, and other needle use endanger our health and might thus disqualify us from being able to donate blood. As we have noted, the preservation of life is of ultimate importance in Judaism, and being able to donate blood regularly is a relatively simple yet important way to help in this mission.

Despite all the proper care we take of our bodies—despite proper nutrition and exercise, the avoidance of unsafe health practices, and regular check-ups with our doctors—medical conditions occasionally arise, warranting our attention and requiring the use of medicine. Inevitably, we all face one condition or another (and sometimes multiple conditions!). We read in Psalms 90:10 that "Seventy are the years of a person's life, eighty if they are strong." Even in the Bible, human beings and the human body were never meant to last an eternity.

There are a number of biblical figures who lived extremely long lives. The longest is Methuselah, who, as we are told in Genesis 5:27, lived 969 years. As one would expect, scholarly biblical analysis looks at these numbers as symbolic. Even Moses lived to "120 years" (Deuteronomy 5:25). There is a Jewish tradition of wishing someone a life of 120 years because that was how long Moses lived. (How interesting it is that, although people generally live much longer now than in generations past, the oldest people still only approach the 120-year mark, but virtually never exceed it. This "outermost" limit has not changed substantially over the years.) As with even the greatest of Biblical figures, medical conditions unavoidably arise over time. At some point, we get sick, and we must begin to accept the inevitability of our eventual demise.

Gaining Jack's Compliance

My goal as Jack's physician is for him to live as long as he can, with as few ailments as possible. Importantly and ideally, Jack should be a partner in this endeavor. There is an abundance of information available to him in this regard. If he doesn't care to read books on how he can become healthier and improve his chances of staying healthy, there is a wealth of information online. The American Heart Association (americanheart.org) and the Mayo Clinic (mayoclinic.com) are two internet sites that he can easily navigate.

Through a combination of lifestyle changes and, if necessary, medication, Jack can expect to improve his chances of being relatively free of activity-limiting disorders. First, though, he must get beyond two hurdles. He must overcome the mental hurdle of denying his problem and accept the need for medication, a better diet, and the cessation of cigarette smoking. And he must overcome physical hurdles that keep him inactive.

Given Jack's reluctance to take medicine, reluctance to adhere to a medical regimen may prove to be a major obstacle in his treatment. An article in the *New England Journal of Medicine* reviewed the issue of patient compliance with instructions to take medicine. It was found that from one quarter to one half of all patients do not take medicine as prescribed (Osterberg, L. et al., 353[2005]:487). In some groups of patients, such as those with financial issues and those with a limited ability to understand and remember why, how, and when to take medicine, the figure is even higher. While many factors play a role in predicting those patients who will take their medication as prescribed and those who will not be compliant, Jack's attitude toward his condition certainly places him in an at-risk group for noncompliance.

Acquiring a Healthy Attitude Toward Medicine

Before Jack can be considered successfully treated, he must accept the proposition that the cost of medicine is a good investment. Then, he must remember to take his medicine each day, accepting the fact that he has a dangerous condition that does not cause him to feel sick in any way. Even before all of this though, there is yet another issue with which we must deal. Jack is resistant to the whole notion of requiring "help." He must be made to understand that as inconvenient as it may be to have to constantly take medicine and get checked at the doctor's office, he will be better able to enjoy life and achieve whatever his life's goals may be if he takes care of his body.

Accepting our own vulnerability to illness and our eventual mortality is difficult for all of us. As a group, teenagers are especially known for their reckless behavior, perhaps in part due to their inability to foresee an end to their lives. But as we grow older and mature, we inevitably begin to see and feel the effects of aging, necessitating a change in our daily health habits and routines. As we have seen, this change often means that we require one or more medications for long periods of time. The good news is that with the continuing advancements in the fields of medicine and pharmacology, the average age of our population continues to increase and the quality of our lives improves. Jack can and should expect no less.

In the course of one of our conversations, Jack made an interesting comment. "I hate to give in and have to take medicine," he said. By using the term "give in," he indicated that by taking medication for his blood pressure he was showing a sign of weakness. "You're not 'giving in,'" I told him. "You're using all the measures that are at your disposal to fight this condition. Rather than look upon the taking of medicine as a sign of weakness, you should look at it as a sign of strength—a tool in your arsenal to fight high blood pressure and to avoid its complications."

If Jack were to assume more responsibility for his own care and acquire more healthy habits—exercising more regularly, eliminating his use of cigarettes, and consuming fewer calories and less alcohol, he would be showing strength and self-control. Perhaps if Jack becomes more assertive and proactive with respect to his health habits, he might indeed be able to avoid the use of medicine for his blood pressure. For now though, he should be grateful that such medications are available to him.

In Judaism, the longer we are of healthy mind and body, the more of God's work we are able to do. Caring for our bodies—our gift—is an essential step in doing His work.

<hr />

APPLYING JEWISH TEACHING

Our body—this mechanical vessel that carries around our soul—is on loan to you for but a short time. You owe it to yourself, your loved ones, and your Creator to preserve your health to the greatest extent possible.

Medications and other forms of health care are nothing short of miraculous, divine gifts. Rather than considering their use a sign of weakness, the fact that you have this arsenal at your disposal is a sign of your strength.

Whatever goals you have in life can more likely be achieved if you are able to preserve and optimize your physical and emotional health.

PART TWO

COPING WITH OTHER CHALLENGES OF LIVING

CHAPTER 5

⊸⊸⊷⊷

THE "SANDWICH" GENERATION: WHEN LIFE SEEMS TO DEMAND TOO MUCH

Marcia's Case: *"Sometimes my heart races and I feel all closed in."*

Marcia's family doctor referred her to me for a heart examination. An uncomfortable awareness of her heartbeat was the source of Marcia's concern. Her doctor had referred a number of patients to me for the same problem, and Marcia hoped that I would be able to handle her problem easily. Though her problem proved to be quite simple to diagnose, it would turn out to be much more difficult to treat, and not necessarily in a medical sense.

Symptoms

Marcia was experiencing palpitations—a symptomatic awareness of the heartbeat that is usually uncomfortable. Sometimes this symptom is caused by a heightened consciousness of an otherwise normal cadence of the heart. At other times, the awareness can be caused by an actual irregularity of the heart's rhythm, usually caused by premature beats—an "impatience" of one or the other of the heart's chambers. This condition often occurs in otherwise normal hearts, and when this is the case, the premature beats do not represent any danger. A reduction in caffeine, decongestants, or alcohol can often help lessen the frequency of these premature beats. Most patients are relieved once they are reassured that the premature beats are not harmful and do not indicate heart disease. When particularly bothersome, these premature beats can be treated with medication to lessen the symptoms.

In Marcia's case, she did not seem to be having an irregularity of the cadence of the heart's rhythm. Rather, she often felt as though her heart was, in her words, "pounding out of my chest," as though it were "about to explode." This would usually happen when all was quiet, such as when she was trying to go to sleep. Awareness of the pounding, though, would also plague Marcia at random times during the day, usually with no obvious precipitating cause. Her exam was quite normal, as was her blood pressure and all of her laboratory studies. She did not have any apparent heart problem; her symptoms seemed to be caused by other factors.

Once specific medical causes had been ruled out, I concluded that Marcia's symptoms were most likely due to an internal environment in which the heart was being driven by excessive adrenaline. The heart was behaving as though it was in a race, even when Marcia was not physically active. Often, this occurrence is the result of stress or anxiety. In Marcia's case, it didn't take much detective work to discover the source of her symptoms.

Marcia's Issues

Marcia's job was undeniably taxing. An account executive for an advertising company, she felt that she was under much pressure to bring in more business. Furthermore, her family's finances caused her much concern. Her husband worked for a high-tech company outside Dallas that had been periodically laying off workers for some time. His job constantly seemed to be on the verge of disappearing. Would he find another comparable job? Would he need to relocate? Did Marcia and her husband have enough savings to weather any temporary loss of income? These questions haunted Marcia constantly with no clear answers.

Marcia was forty-two years old and had two children, ages ten and fourteen. Like most children, they had issues involving school, friends, and activities. Her widowed mother lived nearby and had increasingly demanding needs and health issues. She required much of Marcia's attention, and Marcia worried frequently about her. There seemed to be a never-ending list of doctor's visits, errands, and inconvenient trips to her mother's apartment to help with meals and laundry. Attempts to convince her mother to move into an assisted living arrangement had thus far met fierce resistance. Mom was determined to remain "independent," though actually she was quite dependent on Marcia. Marcia's only brother lived out of state and, while he was supportive, the burden of caring for their mother fell on Marcia's shoulders.

Marcia's work day began in a tense environment and was followed by dinner preparation. Dinner itself was often chaotic and a cacophony of television and telephones. To make matters worse, the family dinner hour often resembled a restaurant. Members of the family ate at different times, depending on school activities and work schedules. There were then school and homework issues, the nightly call to mother that was fraught with the health concern of the day, and, time permitting, maybe some uninterrupted time with her husband. Marcia expressed that she hadn't given him enough attention and support during this time of his occupational uncertainty.

I suggested to Marcia that we monitor her heart during a normal day. The device we would use could be kept for a month, recording her heart rhythm at the touch of a button. Marcia could thus record her heart's cadence whenever she felt palpitations. Sure enough, though her symptoms were frequent, her heart rhythm during these times was quite normal—just a modest speeding up of her typical heart rate. Why was this happening? Was this a serious heart condition? Was her heart "giving out" as she expressed to me? Or was this simply a case of stress and constant tension manifesting itself through the body? Was Marcia's heart saying "ouch" and telling Marcia that there was a problem here that needed attention?

Medical Diagnosis

Marcia was in the "sandwich generation." She had responsibilities as a child, as a parent, and as a wife, each requiring much time and energy. Added to these pressures, she was also dealing with her own issues of work and of financial uncertainty. She questioned whether she and her husband were saving enough for the future. In my judgment, her many sources of stress conspired to cause her symptoms.

Marcia's symptoms were psychosomatic. That is, her "psyche" (pertaining to the brain) was expressing itself in a "somatic" (pertaining to the body) form. The body will often find a way to "express itself" when the psyche is hurting. Some might react to this mountain of tension with headaches; others with abdominal cramps or sleep disturbances. In Marcia's case, constant strain and pressure resulted in palpitations. We often associate the term psychosomatic with imagined illness, but it actually denotes real illness or physical findings caused by psychic issues.

At times, psychosomatic illness can be quite dangerous. The connection between emotional stress and illness in general has been the subject of entire books (Freeman). Asthma, digestive conditions, and headaches are but a few of the physical and symptomatic manifestations of emotional strain. Similarly, stress, job strain, and family loss have been correlated with heart disease (Dimsdale, J.E., *Journal of the Amercian College of Cardiology* 51[2008]:1237; Zipes). Further, studies have shown that after a heart attack, patients with depression have a less promising health outlook than do those with a more positive and optimistic attitude. In Marcia's case, anxiety related to her home and work environment clearly caused her palpitations and might eventually cause even more serious health problems.

One option I had as Marcia's physician was to use a medication to slow the heart down artificially—in essence, an anti-adrenaline medication. However, this would treat merely the symptom and not the cause. The better option would be to treat the ultimate cause of the syptoms—Marcia's internal environment, in which stress was in abundance.

THE JEWISH RESPONSE

Although Marcia has many reasons to feel fortunate, it seemed to her that virtually every aspect of her life was a source of stress—her children, her parent, her work, and perhaps even her family's finances, given her husband's tenuous job status.

Can we help Marcia cope? Fortunately, there is much in the Jewish tradition that can provide useful guidance for each of the sources of stress in Marcia's life.

Marcia's Mother

The first source of Marcia's stress to consider involves her mother. Judaism commands us to honor our parents. The Hebrew word for "honor" can also mean "respect" or "dignify." It is never, however, translated as simply "obey." Adult children often assume responsibility for the well being of their elderly and infirm parents. They become so involved in their care that the usual parent/child roles become reversed. In effect, the children take over the role normally played by the parent. This assumption of responsibility is encouraged in teachings of the Talmud (Judaism's Oral Law that was eventually codified), which outlines behavioral standards of a child toward the parent (Kiddushin 31b). The Talmud teaches that the child is obligated to help a parent when the need arises.

Young parents understand that their responsibility is to do what is best for their children. Sometimes that makes the children happy, and sometimes it doesn't—at least in the short run. When parents become elderly and reach the point where they are, in effect, "parented" by their children, their adult children may have to make similar decisions about what is in the parents' best interest, even if the parents don't readily agree.

We must thus be respectful of our parents and of their dignity by assuring that they are well cared for, seeking living arrangements for them that provide for their increasing needs. But while assuring that her mother's safety, nutrition, and medical needs are provided for, Marcia's responsibility does not necessarily extend to enduring long nightly telephone calls discussing what had become a daily litany of her mother's problems and complaints.

Still, Marcia needs to remember that how she acts toward her mother will have an impact on her own children; she must, therefore, continue to serve as an exemplary model. A parable is told in the Talmud (Ta'anit 5b–6a) about a tired and hungry traveler who eats from a tree and rests in the tree's cool shade. He wishes to bless the tree, but the tree is already hearty, providing fruit and shade. The traveler thus blesses the tree by praying that its shoots will be just like the "mother" tree. For the tree, that would be the ultimate blessing. Similarly, a child who provides for and loves an old and ill parent would indeed be blessed by having children who behave as their parent behaved. Whether or not she is aware of it, Marcia serves as an example and an inspiration to her children; her reward for proper behavior toward her mother will hopefully be that her children will behave similarly toward her when the time comes.

Marcia's Children

The second source of Marcia's stress involves her children and a chaotic home schedule that results, in part, from their needs. The rabbis who are quoted in the Talmud teach that parents are required to teach (or acquire for) our children three things:

1. A good Jewish education
2. A trade, skill, or profession by which they will be able to sustain themselves economically (which for most of us means assuring and supporting their education)
3. The ability to swim (Kiddushin 29a, 30b)

The last requirement is a bit puzzling, both for its specificity, and because of how it relates (or doesn't relate) to the other two. One interpretation is that we are obligated as parents to teach our children how to cope with and thrive in a number of challenging situations. The best way to do this is to provide for them practical experience, first under guidance and supervision. Gradually they will develop competence and confidence. We can readily understand how this relates to the importance of a parent teaching children various chores in the home. One day, of course, the children will be living independently and the skills learned at home will become valuable. While the tasks being taught need to be age-appropriate, there is certainly no reason Marcia couldn't begin teaching some of these household skills (cooking, laundry, cleaning, and so forth) to her children.

As a working mother, Marcia could then reasonably expect the children to use some of these skills to benefit the entire family. Doing these chores would help teach responsibility to her children, easing one of the burdens that cause her stress. The children in turn become justifiably proud of their contribution to the family.

Most importantly, Marcia needs to keep the big picture in mind and be grateful, rather than burdened, by her family. I served my community as a youth sports coach for many years. I now give a talk each fall to fledging youth-basketball coaches. Most of the talk centers on ordering uniforms, organizing practice, and other mundane aspects of coaching with which new coaches are unfamiliar. However, I conclude my talk by telling the coaches: "Remember, when you have to rush home from work so that you have time for dinner before practice, when your afternoon seems harried because of this commitment, and when you must give up part of your weekend to coach while your buddies are golfing or watching football, YOU are the lucky one! What you are doing has much meaning and is of lasting value to your child and your team. So be happy and be proud of yourself. Make it a good experience for all involved, especially you—you deserve it."

Having two healthy and happy children at home should be a source of much pride and pleasure to Marcia. She now deserves and requires a setting and a state of mind in which this pleasure can be realized. In honoring her mother, engaging in employment, and raising two children, Marcia deserves to enjoy the satisfaction and blessing of a happy home.

Adding to Marcia's level of stress is the chaos and noise that the dinner hour represents. The Jewish tradition offers a way to minimize this lack of peace and order. The Biblical account of creation teaches us that God created the world in six days. On the seventh day, God rested, ceasing all creative activity. Thus, God fashioned the first Shabbat, the first Sabbath. If our great and powerful God needed a day off after working, we mere mortals need the same.

Concept of the Sabbath

Author Thomas Cahill, in *The Gifts of the Jews*, refers to the concept of a Sabbath as one of the greatest contributions that the Jews gave to the entire world. Indeed, it is a unique concept that can improve the quality of everyone's life. People may apply the concept in different ways, but we all need a way and a time for refreshing ourselves, recharging our batteries, and renewing our souls, in order to have the energy required to fulfill our responsibilities at work, at home, and at leisure.

Perhaps Rabbi Jonathan Sacks puts it best:

> Shabbat is the holy time of a people that found truth in time. The ancient world had holy places, holy objects, and holy people. But the first thing the Bible calls holy is time itself: "God blessed the seventh day and made it holy" (Genesis 2:3). So Shabbat became our monument of eternity in the midst of time, our glimpse of a world at peace under the sovereignty of God. Within the cycle of the week it creates a delicate rhythm of action and reflection, making and enjoying, running and standing still. Without that pause, Jews might never have continued the journey. Still today, without Shabbat, we risk making the journey while

missing the view. It is Judaism's great messianic
institution. (Sacks, 141)

In many ways, the concept of a Sabbath is much like sleep.
Although scientists are uncertain about the physiological effects of
sleep, we cannot survive without it. Similarly, those of us who strive
to observe the Sabbath laws may not be aware of the benefits gained
in body and soul. However, we find ourselves refreshed, renewed,
and better prepared to face the coming week after observing a full
day of Sabbath rest and reflection. Choosing to restrict our activities,
concentrating on the amazing fact of our existence for one day a
week may result in our interacting in more meaningful ways with
those around us. It may also help us appreciate our small, but very
important, role in a very large universe.

The great twentieth century Jewish philosopher and teacher
Abraham Joshua Heschel refers to the Sabbath as a "sanctuary
in time." As did Rabbi Sacks, Heschel reminds us that, "Jews
have not preserved the ancient monuments, they have retained
the ancient moments" (Heschel, *Man Is Not Alone*, 162). And
even the "secular" Israeli author Ahad Ha'am wrote, "More than
the Jews have kept the Sabbath, the Sabbath has kept the Jews."

Since observing Sabbath helps Jews cope with the many
demands of our increasingly complex lives, perhaps Marcia
and her family can extrapolate the concept, applying it to
their unique needs. Why not make dinnertime a "sanctuary in
time" for the family? Marcia's family may learn to enjoy a
tranquil time together by turning off the television, letting the
answering machine handle any incoming telephone messages,
and arranging a time when everyone can agree to sit together for
this one meal.

There may be some occasions when this is not possible, but
why not have a scheduled time when the family can sit quietly
together and enjoy each other while eating dinner and recounting

the day's events? Dinner would thus be transformed from simply a hunger-relieving interlude that interrupts an otherwise nonstop schedule into a valued family get-together.

Stress Involving Work and Finances

Another of Marcia's stressors is her situation at work. The rabbis understood the importance of making a living, called *parnassah*, and interpreted many rules with enough flexibility to make it easier for people with difficult financial circumstances to make ends meet. A beautiful value expressed in a section of the Talmud called Pirkei Avot (The Ethics of our Fathers) may help us understand another side of this coin. *Aizehu ashir*? *Hasameach b'chelko* (Who is wealthy? One who is happy with his/her portion) (Pirkei Avot 4:1).

This verse from Pirkei Avot tells us that it is good to be happy with what we have. We don't have to struggle to "keep up with the Joneses." Our American culture, sometimes to our benefit and sometimes to our detriment, is extremely consumerist. Far too much value is placed on what we have rather than on what we are. Jewish teachings do not emphasize nor even mention "things" as a source of happiness. Consumer items that are new today are old tomorrow. The acquisition of material goods should not become an end in itself.

Marcia and her husband may benefit from revisiting what is important to them and simplifying their lives. While we don't know the spending habits of Marcia's family, it might help them to "downsize"—to reduce the pressure of maintaining their level of income to match their expenses and consumption. An oft-repeated adage is that no one who faces imminent death thinks, "I should have spent more time at the office." Marcia does not necessarily need to quit her job, but she should at least strive to minimize work-related tension. A reconsideration of her family's expenses and financial goals may help in this regard.

Whatever Marcia envisions in her future, she certainly wouldn't want to look back with regret to this time in her life. To help avoid this regret, she needs to take more time to "smell the roses," relishing this irreplaceable time in the lives of her children, appreciating her good health, and embracing the enveloping love of her mother and her husband.

Certainly, we all encounter stressful situations in our lives that cannot be easily eliminated. Understanding our obligations to our loved ones while not excessively worrying about our own station in life reduces stress. Similarily creating "sanctuaries in time" to enjoy our blessings can go a long way toward reducing our stress level and its resulting symptoms. Marcia is a devoted mother, wife, and daughter, certainly deserving this enjoyment.

APPLYING JEWISH TEACHING

Create sanctuaries in time during which special people and special activities can be enjoyed and appreciated in an uninterrupted way.

Do not allow sources of pride, pleasure, and love to become primarily sources of stress. Take a step back, fulfill your vital responsibilities, and unburden yourself of those tasks that are less important.

To the extent possible, keep the importance of material goods in their proper perspective. "Things" are not enduring sources of happiness and fulfillment.

CHAPTER 6

TROUBLED RELATIONSHIPS AND THEIR EFFECT ON HOW WE FEEL

Pat's Case: *"I had chest pain today at work."*

Pat certainly was loyal to her job. In her eighth year as a nurse in the same pediatric office, she spent her day helping to care for children by screening phone calls from worried parents and by assisting the doctor in the children's examinations. She also made an effort trying to avoid Fran, who sat at the front desk, answering the telephone and scheduling appointments. We'll discuss more about the relationship between Pat and Fran later.

Symptoms

An internist referred Pat to me because of chest pain. She experienced discomfort in the central portion of her chest, causing concern that it might be related to her heart. The coronary arteries supply the heart muscle with blood, delivering oxygen and nutrients. When these vessels become constricted, blood can't pass through in adequate amounts. The result is discomfort, known as angina. The cause of this constriction, or gradual closure, is arteriosclerosis—hardening of the arteries. The possibility that Pat had this potentially dangerous condition led her internist to request the appointment with me.

Medical Testing

Hardening of the arteries (arteriosclerosis) can be the result of diabetes, high blood pressure, cigarettes, high cholesterol, bad genes, or any combination of these "risk factors." As with most medical conditions, bad luck also plays a role. The discomfort experienced by the patient is most often caused by exertion. The oxygen requirements of the heart are less when we are at rest than when we are active. The more active we are at any given moment, the greater the oxygen need. When the process of arteriosclerosis is advanced, almost any form of exertion can cause discomfort. Even stress, with its attendant increase in heart rate and blood pressure, can trigger anginal pain in some people.

Pat's discomfort occurred most often at work, when there was at least some physical activity. But she was able to exercise at home or at the gym without any discomfort at all. Pat was a nonsmoker, and other than a mildly elevated cholesterol level, she had none of the traditional factors that cause hardening of the arteries. Was this a case of typical heart-related pain, or was something else causing her discomfort? A stress test was performed in the office, during which Pat exercised while being monitored.

Cardiac stress testing on patients can be performed by using a treadmill—a machine that enables one to walk in place, using an incline if desired, while the heart's electrical activity is observed. The test can help detect instances where hardening of the arteries is the cause of the patient's chest discomfort. Often though, imaging of the heart in some form is also done, using either ultrasound or radioisotopes. These imaging techniques enhance the accuracy of the test. Pat had an ultrasound study (an exercise echocardiogram) during which she exercised to a high level of activity and had no suggestion of an obstruction in her coronary vessels. Though she was relieved, the nagging issue that brought her to my office in the first place—her chest pain—remained.

The Root of the Problem

Since Pat brought up the subject of her work environment at the time of her first office visit, I mentioned it again after her stress test. Pat claimed to enjoy what she was doing and liked the physician with whom she worked. She believed she was of much value to the families who came to the office and felt she was well paid. Lately, however, she found herself less patient with the children who came to the office, admitting to being a bit irritable with the parents. Although she had known no other line of work, she began to wonder whether or not this was the right environment for her. She also admitted to feeling much stress from a wounded relationship with Fran, a secretary in the office. She seemed relieved to be able to discuss all this; it seemed that her emotions had been bottled up for a long time.

The sequence with Fran is probably familiar to us all. Fran took some of Pat's words the wrong way, creating some strain between them. Pat then spoke additional words to a third party—words that ultimately (and perhaps inevitably) found their way back to Fran, who then chose to ignore Pat. Silence led to hard feelings on both sides, and a vicious cycle began. This resulted in more words to third parties, more animosity, and less communication. Pat found herself withdrawing not only from interactions with Fran, but also from those with others in the office. In the tense environment in which Pat found herself, physical distress is common. This tension can be expressed as headaches, sleep disturbances, abdominal pain, or as was the case with Pat, chest pain. As emotional stress builds and persists, the body's distress eventually finds an outlet—an internal manifestation letting the patient know that "something is awry."

When a person experiences physical symptoms with no objective abnormalities, we say that these symptoms are "functional" in nature. That is, they are due to the normal functioning of the body. The symptoms are no less real than if they are caused by real organic disease, but there is one important difference. In cases of inflammatory diseases, circulatory abnormalities, or tumors, normal bodily anatomy and processes are disrupted, resulting in symptoms. Tissue from the body is altered in a damaging way. These changes can often be found by laboratory tests, x-rays, and so forth.

On the other hand, in cases of functional discomfort, no specific pathological findings are to be found. All our diagnostic studies are basically normal. From time to time, we all experience various aches and pains. Certainly, testing must be done to look for specific diseases that can cause these symptoms. Most often, when the testing fails to find an abnormality, the symptoms are probably nothing more than what I call "somatic noise" and can usually be safely ignored.

When repeated examinations fail to find abnormalities and no identifiable cause is found, physicians generally try to reassure the patient that there is nothing harmful in a physical sense. Searching for emotional factors that are at the root of these symptoms can often be quite useful. Emotional stress can make any symptom worse, whether functional in nature or due to real organic illness. Individuals with arthritis, for example, may well have an increase in their symptoms during times of emotional stress. We know that high blood pressure and its attendant signs and symptoms can similarly be affected by emotions. Another example is asthma, which is certainly affected by emotional stress.

In Pat's case, her cardiac testing reassured us that her heart was fine. Her symptoms were quite real, though. At that point, we felt compelled to look to the mind for clues as to why Pat was so physically uncomfortable.

THE JEWISH RESPONSE

This mind-body connection is as old as the Bible, which provides us with examples of physical signs and symptoms resulting from behavioral issues. For example, we read in the Torah (Numbers 12:1–10) that Moses's sister Miriam was upset that Moses married a "foreign" woman. She and Aaron "spoke against Moses." Soon after this transgression, and perhaps as punishment by God, Miriam was stricken with a case of leprosy. Moses prayed on her behalf, and she was healed after seven days of isolation. While we do not know the exact details of what transpired between Pat and her co-workers, she does seem to have been adversely affected in a physical sense by her strained relationship with Fran.

Relationships and Improper Speech

We are also told (Deuteronomy 10:16) to "Circumcise the foreskin of your heart and be no more stiff-necked." This metaphor shows that the heart is capable of growing a "covering" that deadens its sensations, making us even more insensitive and perhaps stubborn as well. This metaphorical covering, this insensitivity to the feeling of others and to God's teachings, must be removed before the difficult work of relationship repair can be started and we can feel whole again. The task is simple to understand, but certainly not easy to accomplish.

The Jewish holiday of *Yom Kippur* (Day of Atonement) is the holiest day of the year, when Jews confess all their sins before God and in the presence of their entire congregation. One of the prayers on this day is confessional in nature—the *Al Chet* prayer meaning "for the sin which we have committed by . . ." The prayer lists a number of transgressions that are likely to have been committed by the congregants during the course of the prior year. The vast majority of those sins are committed by improper and sinful speech such as gossiping and lying.

Harmful Words

One of the sins for which we ask forgiveness is called lashon hara (the evil tongue). Interestingly, the truth or untruth of what we say is irrelevant. If we speak negatively about someone, even if it is true, then we are guilty of the sin of lashon hara. This may also involve a situation in which even flattering speech may be harmful. If, for example, such speech is said about someone to their "enemy," the enemy will be reminded of their ill will towards the subject. We thus cause and perpetuate negative thoughts, and so are guilty because of what would seem to be an innocent utterance. This specific kind of lashon hara is called *ona'at devarim* (words that cause pain).

While one might commonly hear the adage, "sticks and stones may break my bones, but names will never hurt me," Jews don't believe this. We understand the tremendous power of words, for the Bible tells us that it was simply by speaking words that God created the entire world. And so we understand that we, too, as beings created in God's image, can use words to either build or destroy—perhaps not entire worlds, but certainly a person's self esteem. Jews are taught that people must be very careful with the words we speak and how we use them.

In fact, Jewish law prohibits what is called *malbin et hapanim* (whitening the face). The prohibition informs us that embarrassing someone to the point that the blood leaves the face (whitening, or making the afflicted person appear ashen) is tantamount to murdering them (i.e., "drawing" the blood").

There are, however, some exceptions to these rules. If someone is about to enter into a contract with another person, whether for marriage or business, we are allowed to say things that are true but unflattering about that person. This is ture provided we have direct knowledge of, or experience with, them. The knowledge or experience we impart may help avert a hurtful, or at least uninformed, contractual relationship.

Healing Words

On the other hand, some well-placed words of good will can have an unexpectedly beneficial effect. When I was in college, Larry was a classmate of mine who, planned or not, helped repair a relationship between me and his roommate, Tom. Larry was speaking with me when I mentioned that there had been a bit of a chill in the relationship between Tom and me. I felt that Tom didn't care to be around me, though we had had little actual contact. In retrospect, I was probably just a bit hypersensitive. "Gee, he speaks well of you, Joel," was all Larry said. The relationship between Tom and me was transformed by these very simple words. Immediately, I behaved differently towards Tom, and perhaps not surprisingly, Tom behaved differently in return. How surprising to me still, that seven simple words spoken by a third party dramatically changed a relationship.

An example of just such behavior in the Bible involves Aaron, the first high priest and brother of Moses. The Talmud often speaks of Aaron as being a pursuer of peace. How did he achieve this? When he knew two people were feuding, he would first approach one and say, "So and so says he is really sorry for his actions. Because of his shame, he is waiting for you to approach him, so he can ask your forgiveness." He would then approach the other party to the feud and make the exact same statement, word for word. When the two people met in the street, they would embrace and resume peaceful relations.

Dealing Directly with Those We Have Harmed

The very first service that begins the Yom Kippur prayer service is called *Kol Nidre* (All Vows), whereby we ask God to annul "all vows" that we were not able to keep. This applies only to sins committed against God—mainly ritual activity and prayers. These are called *bein adam l'makon* (between a person and God). Significantly though, for any sins committed against other people, we learn that we must first deal directly with the people against whom we sinned. These sins are called *bein adam l'chaveiro* (between a person and his fellow human beings). We learn that we must first ask to be forgiven by the individual against whom we sinned before we can ask God to forgive us for those sins. (This was, of course, long before any "Twelve-step" programs, such as in Alcoholics Anonymous, existed. As we know, the AA program uses just such an approach.)

Accepting the wisdom of the Jewish tradition would be beneficial to Pat, thinking about sins she may have committed in the realm of "evil tongue," and determining whether an apology to Fran is in order for some of the things she said. That might break the ice and restore a more positive relationship.

Jews are also commanded to "seek peace and pursue it," one of the only biblical commandments to employ two different verbs, indicating to us both its importance and the importance of taking swift and decisive action. We are not to wait until things have festered.

If Pat can't bring herself to discuss the issue directly with Fran, there is another option. Maybe she can at least be pleasant to Fran, hoping to begin a positive cycle of good words and deeds, leading to mutually improved feelings. While the more direct approach follows Jewish teachings, this alternate plan has underpinnings in the Bible as well.

Constructive Actions and Attitudes

When the Israelites received God's laws from Moses, we are told they responded, "All that the Lord has spoken, *na'aseh ve-nishma*, we will do and we will hear" (Exodus 24:7). This response has often been taken to mean, "We will do and we will understand." Why does "doing" come before "understanding"? Daniel Gordis explains:

> Why should performance of God's commands precede understanding them? Shouldn't understanding come first? In what has become a pivotal characteristic of Judaism, Jewish tradition insists that understanding need not come first. Tradition suggests that the Torah's peculiar language is instructive; it is no accident that the people first promise to act and then say they will understand. The Torah's insight is that in the Jewish world of religion, study and meaning, the feelings, the faith, and the spirituality we seek often follow behaviors specifically designed to elicit them. Jewish faith and Jewish spirituality do not come out of thin air, insists Jewish tradition. They come out of uniquely Jewish behaviors designed to let them grow and develop. (Gordis, 72)

In a validation of this biblical verse, University of Virginia psychology professor Timothy Wilson writes:

> Aristotle suggested that we acquire virtues by first having put them in action . . . We become just by the practice of just actions, self-controlled by exercising self-control, and courageous by performing acts of courage . . . As suggested by nineteenth century psychologist William James, the more frequently people perform a behavior, the more habitual it becomes, requiring little effort or conscious attention. One of the most enduring lessons of social psychology is that behavior change often *precedes* (italics the authors') changes in attitudes and feelings. (Wilson, 211)

Pat's words and behavior may set in motion a cascade of improved feelings for all parties involved. As we discussed earlier, the Talmud has a saying in Pirkei Avot—*miztvah goreret mitzvah; aveirah goreret aveirah* (Deeds of good behavior will generate still more deeds of good behavior) (Pirkei Avot 4:2). Similarly, the act of transgressing—sinful behavior—will lead to more transgressions. Again, while it is much easier said than done, the more we follow God's commandments to be ethical and benevolent human beings, the better our lives and our behavior will subsequently be.

A Different Approach Toward Work

This lesson pertains to Pat's interactions not only with her coworkers, but also with the patients with whom she comes in contact. Not only is the value of work emphasized in Judaism numerous times in our teachings, but also Pat's work in particular lends itself to the performance of good deeds. She didn't need to be reminded that in her daily encounters as a pediatric nurse, she is visited all day by frightened children (and frightened parents!). She is involved in many situations in which she can spread kindness.

Pat needs a paradigm shift in her thinking and approach. Instead of looking upon each patient as a chore to be dealt with, she needs to view each office visit and phone call as an opportunity to help—to make a positive impact on someone's life, however briefly. Her work provides repeated opportunities to soothe and reassure. Jews are taught to "receive everyone with a cheerful face" (Pirkei Avot 1:15). Performing *g'milut chasadim* (acts of loving-kindness) can have a positive impact not only on the patients with whom Pat comes in contact, but also on Pat herself.

In his work, *God in Search of Man*, Abraham Joshua Heschel reminds us that: "We believe that every hour is endowed with the power to lend meaning to—or withhold meaning from—all other hours. It is not by the rare act of greatness that character is determined, but by everyday actions, by a constant effort to rend our callousness. It is constancy that sanctifies. Judaism is an attempt to place all of life under the glory of ultimate significance, to relate all scattered actions to the One" (Heschel, 218, 384).

So Pat is fortunate to be in a position where she can have a positive impact on so many people in the course of her daily work. If she can simply carry herself in a proud and happy way, looking for ways to spread comfort and good cheer to her coworkers as well as her patients, perhaps much of her chest discomfort will abate.

APPLYING JEWISH TEACHING

Words are not only powerful but irretrievable. Choose them very carefully, and give great consideration to how they are used.

Every interaction we have is an opportunity to spread goodness and kindness. Instead of approaching work and the mundane tasks in your life as burdens, consider them as occasions in which you can make yourself and others just a bit happier.

When a change in attitude seems too difficult to achieve, try to effect this change by remembering that a change in behavior can actually bring about a change in attitude in yourself and in others.

CHAPTER 7

DEALING WITH UNFULFILLED DREAMS AND DECLINING RELEVANCE

Ravi's Case: *"I'm tired and just don't feel good."*

On the surface, Ravi's yearly checkup seemed to be routine. He had coronary bypass surgery four years ago and had done quite well. An exercise study was performed to be sure his coronary grafts were functioning as expected. Although Ravi had not called the office to report any symptoms of illness, he was not happy with how he was feeling, and his visit on this day would include more than just the test on his heart.

Before he became a patient, Ravi and I knew each other through youth sports—our children played on the same team. Ravi had come to this country as a child, brought by his parents from South Asia to escape the civil and religious strife that was engulfing his country at the time. A civil engineer, he was now sixty-two years old, only three years away from his company's retirement age.

In the years I knew him, Ravi exhibited a deep sense of honor with a strong social conscience. He repeatedly expressed gratitude for the opportunities made available to him in this country. Ravi appeared financially secure, and he had two grown daughters and several grandchildren. His wife accompanied him to the office for his exercise study.

Symptoms

Ravi did not have exertional chest discomfort during his usual exercise routine, which consisted of a brisk walk several times each week and some light weightlifting. His breathing was fine, and he had no complaints related to his heart. However, he did note a couple of things that were bothersome to him: periodically, he found himself taking a deep breath and wondered if he had a lung problem. Additionally, he noted that sometimes he was aware of his heartbeat, often able actually to hear each impulse in his ears. Ravi also complained of some nondescript joint aching and infrequent mild cramps in his abdomen. Finally, Ravi looked at me with rather sad eyes and said, "I'm tired and I just don't feel good."

Medical Diagnosis

While most of Ravi's feelings and complaints can be explained physiologically, they constitute what I frequently call "somatic noise"—an awareness of various goings-on in the body that most of us experience from time to time. These feelings are not associated with actual illness and can be contrasted with somatic signals that often signify actual disease.

Many if not most people have some of these minor sensations from time to time; they represent nothing more than the normal workings of the body. The amount of "noise" we are able to report correlates with our own level of awareness of our body's workings. When they come into our awareness to the point of distraction, though, it sometimes means that there is a relative lack of other stimuli to occupy our minds. These other stimuli can range from work to play, but without them, our minds may focus on these internal sensations—the noise. And there is certainly no shortage of noise that each of us can experience in a given day.

When a patient comes to an office visit with a number of somatic complaints, a specific disorder is often present, and it is up to the clinician to diagnose the particular illness causing the symptoms. Occasionally, people who are troubled emotionally come to the office armed with a list of numerous and apparently disconnected symptoms. When generalized fatigue is one of the symptoms, an underlying nonphysical issue is often present. Certainly, a physical exam and some laboratory studies are in order as part of the assessment. In Ravi's case, all of this checked out just fine.

A Wounded Psyche

In all the years I had taken care of him, Ravi had never offered such a variety of complaints. I wondered if maybe the problem was more related to a wounded psyche rather than a wounded body.

Perhaps the problem was not in Ravi's joints, heart, or gastrointestinal tract. Perhaps the problem was more "above the neck." A casual chat with Ravi revealed some clues, especially since I had known him for a number of years. In particular, he expressed some frustration that he had never achieved what he thought he would in his field of work. He once thought about starting his own consulting company, but for whatever reason, it just didn't happen.

Even within his own company, he never rose to an executive level and was frustrated by what he perceived as unfairness and misjudgment on the part of the corporate higher-ups. Now it all seemed too late. He was in his final years with the company and felt that other companies in his field would shy away from hiring him, given his age.

Ravi was a bright, healthy, compassionate man, with productive time available to him. Having worked diligently for long hours and for many years, and having been focused on his family and his job, he hadn't developed hobbies or outside interests. He had not been involved with life outside his family and work. Although he was quite proud of his family, Ravi felt unfulfilled because he had not attained his professional goals.

Additionally, he expressed frustration that although he had a strong social conscience and sense of purpose, he had never translated those feelings into action in any meaningful way. His life had taken a fateful turn when he was brought to this country. Through hard work, he had been able to achieve much in the way of material success. Now he expressed frustration and perhaps some degree of guilt that he hadn't been able to leave more of an impact on society. "What have I done, really?" he once asked me. Further, he was skeptical as to the impact he might be able to make in society at this point in his life. It was clear to me from my conversation with Ravi that the problem was not with his various organ systems. The problem had more to do with his soul.

Erik Erikson, in his famous work, *Childhood and Society*, describes the developmental life cycle of human beings in what he terms the "Eight Ages of Man." The eighth and final stage is "maturity," which is characterized by the struggles between "ego integrity" and "despair." Ravi seems to be a perfect example of such an Eriksonian conflict. On the one hand, he is proud of what he has overcome and accomplished in his life. On the other hand, he seems to be fighting despair that the end of his life is too close, and he hasn't accomplished all that he wanted to or thought that he would.

THE JEWISH RESPONSE

To what standard is a life held in Judaism? Is there a measuring stick—a gauge—against which we can determine if our lives have fulfilled what God expects of us? Yes, in our ancient writings we find just such a test.

Four Questions

In the Talmud (Shabbat 31a) we are taught that each of us will be asked four questions when we die and meet our Maker. The first is, "Were you honest in your business dealings?" Ravi certainly seems to be able to answer yes to this, based on the history we have.

Another question is, "Did you follow the commandment to be fruitful and multiply?" That is, "Did you have a family and concern yourself with its welfare?" Hearing that Ravi did indeed have children and that he seemed to have been a loving and attentive father and husband, we can assume that he can answer this question in the affirmative as well.

"Did you set aside specific times for studying Torah?" is a third question. This can be interpreted as, "Did you make time for your spiritual well-being and for the things you love?" This is where Ravi, and many of us, may come up short. The Jewish philosopher Abraham Joshua Heschel writes in *God in Search of Man,* "If the world is only power to us and we are all absorbed in a gold rush, then the only god we may come upon is the golden calf." We can be so overwhelmed with our careers that many of the other things in our lives fall by the wayside. Sometimes, that can lead to family conflict and even a painful divorce. At the other extreme, we can be overwhelmed by family responsibilities that can affect our work or prevent us from holding certain jobs.

The fourth question we will deal with from this section of the Talmud is *tzipitah lishua,* which is usually translated as "Did you expect salvation?" It might also be translated as "Did you look for ways to save the world?" The concept of *tikun olam*, of repairing the world, is very strong throughout Jewish teaching and is even considered as the reason for our creation by God—to make the world a better place while we are here. Perhaps Ravi would be more fulfilled if he committed himself to helping fix the world and make it a better place. This can be achieved with either philanthropy or by volunteering his time to worthwhile and needy causes.

Some may understand this phrase to mean "Did you have hope for the future?" Perhaps those with hope for the future will be more inclined to make that optimistic vision come true. I doubt that any of us has a positive attitude all the time, but we have more control over our outlook than we might realize. We can also look to the Bible for examples of optimists.

Joseph's Optimism

The biblical Joseph is a good example of an eternal optimist. Joseph was a dreamer as a child, but it seemed that his dreams were going to be his undoing when his brothers became resentful of him (Genesis, Ch. 37). They not only grew tired of hearing about his dreams but also became angry that Joseph was the favorite son of their father Jacob. Incredibly, Joseph went from being his father's favorite to being sold into slavery. Instead of becoming despondent, however, Joseph took advantage of his talent. Eventually, he was sold to Potiphar and worked his way up to a position of authority in Potiphar's home. Apparently, Joseph's rise to power quite impressed Potiphar's wife, who tried numerous times to seduce him (Genesis, Ch. 39).

After she was repeatedly rebuffed by Joseph, she became frustrated and falsely accused him of attempted rape, for which he was again imprisoned. While in jail, Joseph used his powers of dream interpretation for fellow inmates to gain himself some notoriety. When Pharaoh himself had two similar and unsettling dreams, one of Joseph's former cellmates remembered his unusual gift and recommended him to Pharaoh. Joseph was immediately summoned before Pharaoh and interpreted both dreams so well that Pharaoh offered him a position in the government that might be considered akin to "chief operating officer."

At many points in his life, Joseph could have given up. Instead, he used his positive attitude and his God-given talents in ways that actually led to the realization of his own dreams. Rather than exclusively crediting his own talent and skill for his success, Joseph was mature and spiritual enough at that stage in his life to accept that his good fortune and God's providence played a role in enabling events to work out the way they did.

But this fourth question from our Maker when we die might also have more to do with our life's relevance. Maybe we all want to be able to answer, "Yes, I strove for and expected salvation by doing Your work while I was alive. I tried to make a difference in the world—not just in my work and by raising a family, but also by helping others live better lives. I did this by having a concern for people and acting on this concern in the best way I could."

Author Richard Nelson Bolles is famous for his book *What Color Is Your Parachute?*, about how to conduct a proper job search. Bolles also wrote *The Three Boxes of Life*, which instructs us about how to formulate goals for our lives and work. Each proverbial box represents one phase of our lives: learning (education), work (career), and leisure (retirement). Realizing that most people focus only on the first two phases of their lives, Bolles stresses the importance of balance in one's life among the three areas.

Seeking and Gaining Relevance

Bolles might say that until this time in his life, Ravi had been neglecting the important leisure box. But maybe a fourth box should be added to Bolles's conceptual framework. This box would involve a person's relevance and the meaning of his life. Is your life relevant? Have you made a difference? Is the world better because you have lived? For many people, their careers enable them to answer these questions affirmatively. However, some may approach the end of their working lives with a vague sense of emptiness, the disquieting feeling that their work and their days failed to serve a useful purpose. It seems that as Ravi approaches the end of his working career he finds he has neglected this fourth box. But as we will see, it is not too late.

Perhaps Ravi needs to begin the pursuit of another goal—the goal of being relevant, of being needed. In his book, *Man Is Not Alone*, Heschel writes extensively about this.

> The concern for others is not an extension in breadth but an ascension, a rise. Man reaches a new vertical dimension, the dimension of the holy, when he grows beyond his self-interests, when that which is of interest to others becomes vital to him . . . The only way to avoid despair is to be a need rather than an end. Happiness may be defined as the certainty of being needed. But who is in need of man? The first answer that comes to mind is a societal one . . . There is not a soul on this earth which, however vaguely or rarely, has not realized that life is dismal if not mirrored in something which is lasting . . . The days of our lives are representatives of eternity rather than fugitives, and we must live as if the fate of all of time would totally depend on a single moment. (Heschel, 139, 194, 198, 205)

Ravi, with his strong social conscience, relatively good health, and preserved energy, seems to yearn for relevance. He has achieved financial comfort and has given of himself to his family and company. His frustrations might be transformed into feelings of achievement and worth if he is able to act on his desire to make a difference in society. There was a commercial that ran some years ago for the National Basketball Association and its players that highlighted the community service work performed by its players. The ad features a story told by a former player, Bob Lanier. In the commercial, a boy is walking along the shore, throwing beached starfish back into the ocean. A man walks by the boy, telling him, "You can't help all those fish, son." As the boy tosses yet another fish back into the water he replies, "But I helped that one."

The passer-by saw an insurmountable task. However, the young boy was the embodiment of an ancient Jewish admonition (Pirkei Avot 2:21), "You are not required to complete the task (of healing the world of its ills), yet you are not free to withdraw from it."

The Case of Moses

As for Ravi's sense of disappointment with his career, Judaism can point to a wonderful example of overcoming disappointment and reshaping expectations—that of Moses.

Moses was the greatest leader the people of Israel ever had. He became a good role model because of his attitude, particularly towards the end of his life. After the death of his sister Miriam (Numbers 20:1–13), Moses was understandably upset and ill-tempered. The Israelites, a "stiff-necked" people, lacked water and once again began to grumble. Moses turned to God, who told him what to do to get water. As his people continued their grumbling and complaining, Moses began to lose his patience, yelling at the people, and then striking the rock instead of following God's instructions to speak to the rock. After serving the people as their leader while in Egypt and for their entire sojourn in the desert, Moses heard his punishment for disobeying God. He would not be allowed to lead his people into the Promised Land.

Moses later (Numbers 27:15–23) asked God for the opportunity to appoint his successor, and Joshua was so named. Moses also invested Joshua with the "right of succession" by transferring his power to Joshua in front of all the people, thinking about the people's welfare and suppressing his own emotions. A lesser man might have opted to relinquish his power in a number of other ways. As promised, God allowed Moses to see the Promised Land from the top of Mt. Nebo (Deuteronomy 32:48–52), but not to enter the land.

Moses is a stark example of a person not being able to fulfill his life's goals. This great leader was so exalted that he spoke with God. "Never again did there arise in Israel a prophet like Moses—whom the Lord singled out, face to face" (Deuteronomy 34:10). Yet Moses still didn't get to see all his dreams and goals realized. Despite what must have been great disappointment, Moses didn't let God's decree affect his ability to function as the leader of his people. At the end of Deuteronomy, we find Moses at peace with himself.

A midrash describes Moses's reaction when he found the Israelites worshiping a golden calf. They were spiritually immature and had lost faith in Moses because he had been gone for forty days, and thus they reverted to pagan worship. Moses had carried the tablets containing the Ten Commandments down from Mount Sinai, but upon seeing how the Israelites had lost faith, he smashed the tablets.

The midrash tells us that he then picked up the pieces and kept them. When the Ark that was to hold the tablets of the covenant was finally built and placed in the *Mishkan* (the Holy

Tabernacle), Moses placed the broken pieces alongside the new tablets. The broken tablets were a metaphor for Moses, who seemed to know instinctively the importance of picking up the broken pieces of his life and taking them with him, so that he could overcome their "power" over him.

Ravi's Remaining Years

We all have broken remnants from the histories of our lives. We can learn from them by packing them up, taking them with us, dealing with and ultimately resolving the issues involved. Alternatively, we can let them color our lives so that we never stop feeling broken. Our way of handling life's hurts and disappointments is up to us. As I chat with patients nearing retirement, I commonly find wistfulness for times past—a sense that their hopes and dreams weren't fulfilled. Life's path is strewn with compromises and disappointments. Like our Biblical ancestors, we are imperfect, and our lives are imperfect.

Is it too late for Ravi to have professional dreams? Maybe not—given his relatively good health, he likely still has a number of productive years left to work. If specific actions regarding his career will help ease his mental anguish, it would certainly be better for him to strive and act rather than lament.

Beyond his work, though, there is another realm in which Ravi may find satisfaction. Having expressed gratitude for the opportunities presented to him, maybe it is time for him to take to heart two verses in the Talmud. First, "You are not required to complete the task (of improving conditions in the world), yet you are not free to withdraw from it" (Pirkei Avot 2:21). According to this teaching, we all have an obligation to do our part in healing the world. The second comes from Rabbi Hillel: "If I am not for myself, who will be for me? And if I am only for myself, what am I? And if not now, when?" (Pirkei Avot 1:14). A whole host of opportunities is available in most communities for Ravi to make a difference. It is time for him to deal with his perceived near-empty fourth box of life—the one of meaning and relevance. Rabbi Jonathan Sacks addresses God's call to action:

> Where was God when Cain killed Abel (and, by extension, when all other acts of evil occur in the world)? Where was God when he might have intervened? To this there is one answer. We have been traveling with it since we first met Abraham and his cry at the injustice of the world. Abraham, says the midrash, saw a palace (the world) in flames, God's order threatened by the chaos of mankind. To the question, 'Where is God?' God replies with a question of his own, 'Where are you?'—His first words to Adam and Eve, and to Job. Jewish faith did not die in this question; it was born in it. (Sacks, 188)

So Judaism has much to say to Ravi about how he should be approaching this phase of his life. It begins with the question, "Where are you, Ravi?" While his career at work might be drawing to a close, there will now be time to begin another career—a mission to make his life purposeful. This mission is likely to be meaningful and give him much joy. It might even alleviate some of his bothersome physical symptoms.

APPLYING JEWISH TEACHING

No matter how your days are spent, make those days relevant so that your life will be relevant.

Matter. Make a difference in the world by making a difference in people's lives.

Optimism and hope are powerful sentiments that can be catalysts in the quest to make tomorrow better than today.

Although you may not achieve all the dreams and all the goals you set out for yourself, use those disappointments and shortcomings as an incentive to fulfill other aspirations.

Chapter 8

THE NEED FOR REPENTANCE
AND PERSONAL BOUNDARIES

Lisa's Case: *"It's really no big deal."*

Lisa was not at all what I had expected. I imagined a young woman resentful of authority figures and reluctant to keep her office appointment. Instead, Lisa was personable with a ready smile and solid eye contact. I had envisioned a high school student with a negative attitude toward school and its opportunities. But Lisa was quick to tell me her favorite subjects, history and Spanish. I had anticipated overt tension between the patient and her parent. To my surprise, Lisa and her mother communicated easily and with no apparent animosity toward each other.

I was informed of this consultation earlier in the day by an officer at a detention center where seventeen-year-old Lisa was found to have an irregular pulse. She had apparently been taken into custody because of cocaine use. One of the friends with Lisa when she was apprehended actually required a hospital admission. Lisa now needed to be examined by a cardiologist to see if she had a heart condition.

Lisa was brought to the office by her mother, Judy, a tall, well-dressed woman in her forties. Judy worked as a nurse, and she was familiar with the possible damaging effects of illicit drugs on the heart. Her tense lips and reddened eyes revealed intense distress. She spoke in short, clipped sentences that reflected her deep anxiety, worry, and perhaps anger at Lisa's situation. I briefly interviewed Judy separately and learned that she had been widowed when Lisa was a small girl. Only the previous year had she remarried and, although Lisa seemed to get along well with her new husband, Judy felt that Lisa resented the fact that this new man had "intruded" upon their home.

Judy sensed that Lisa saw her new husband as a competitor for Judy's time and attention. Still, it seemed to Judy that the home setting was quite warm and comfortable, with no overt conflicts or financial stress. Lisa had all the material things she needed, went to a good school, and engaged in extracurricular activities including sports and drama. Judy felt she had provided Lisa with all she needed, including her love and her presence, and she was now devastated at this turn of events.

Lisa was quite engaging during the exam. She told me about her school and her participation in basketball and drama. She also readily discussed her family situation with no hint of strife. Though I certainly don't have a lot of experience with substance abuse, I imagined this was a quite typical picture. From the outside, one would look at Lisa and her situation and wonder, "Why would someone like this possibly get involved with drugs? How could this happen to such a family?" These are questions that are undoubtedly asked each time a situation such as this occurs.

Medical Issues

Lisa had an abnormality on her physical examination beyond the irregular pulse. She had wheezes in her lungs and coughed frequently during the course of the exam. As I discovered during the visit, Lisa also smoked cigarettes. Her mother told me that she had childhood asthma but that this condition had seemed to clear up as she got older. Lisa required the use of an inhaler infrequently, and her participation in activities was unaffected. However, the wheezing was an unmistakable sign of early lung disease.

While an irregular pulse is unusual in a teenager, it may not represent any particular damage to the heart. We would further examine Lisa's heart with an echocardiogram—an ultrasound exam in which the structure and function of the heart could be determined. She would have to make a separate appointment for this exam and would need to come back to the office. I asked Judy if it would be okay with her for me to speak with Lisa alone at the time of that visit. She readily agreed.

The following week, Lisa was back in the office with Judy, and her echocardiogram was normal. Lisa continued to have a somewhat irregular pulse, caused by premature beats of the upper chambers of the heart. While this is unusual in a teenager, my judgment was that it did not represent a serious condition. It was unclear as to whether drugs played a role in this irregularity, but it seemed likely that neither medication nor further examination would be required at this point.

Denial and Its Consequences

As per my earlier conversation with her mother, I asked Lisa to join me in my consultation room so that we might chat privately. Behind closed doors and away from her mother, Lisa was still remarkably at ease and personable.

My impression after speaking with her was that she didn't understand the magnitude of her problem. In fact, she didn't recognize that she had a problem at all. Without delving extensively into her past, I could not gauge how much involvement she had with illicit drugs. But her perception was certainly different from that of the detention officers. Lisa told me, "It's really no big deal." Of note, Lisa told me that she had been with her boyfriend on the night she was picked up by the police and felt that she had been coerced by him and by her other friends to "try new things."

Lisa also downplayed her use of cigarettes, telling me that she only smoked "once in a while." She certainly couldn't smoke at home, so her use of cigarettes was restricted to after school, when she could get away with her friends. She didn't feel that her occasional asthma was made worse by her smoking, since this was a problem that, after all, went back to her early childhood. Since Lisa was still able to engage in her activities without any noticeable breathlessness, she felt that her use of cigarettes was harmless.

Possibly Lisa didn't fully grasp the health implications of drug use. She expressed surprise that her friend had gotten sick and was actually taken to the hospital on the night they were apprehended. Still, Lisa basically felt healthy and felt that her "occasional" forays into the world of drugs was "no big deal." While she acknowledged that cigarette use was potentially harmful, she stated that since she only smoked "a few" cigarettes, it was not now, and would not become, a health issue.

Lisa did not relate to me any obvious issue at home with her new stepfather; in fact, she spoke well of him. Still, she admitted that things had changed a lot at home, especially with respect to the relationship she had with her mother. Given the brief contact I had with Lisa, I recognized the improbability of having much effect on her behavior. This was a project and a process that was clearly going to take many encounters, necessarily spanning many weeks with a professional—one who deals with these issues all the time. Still, every process must have a beginning. I thus felt a responsibility to impart whatever knowledge, advice, and encouragement I could.

Taking into account the various issues involved with Lisa, I felt that she was clearly in denial. She understood the severity of the problem of illicit drug use and its health and legal implications, yet she minimized the importance and the implications of her use of cocaine. She certainly learned about the effects of cigarette smoking, yet she seemed to reject the idea that her asthma and continued wheezing might have been worsened by her smoking. The emotional upheaval that her behavior had caused her mother was quite obvious. Still, she did not take any responsibility for her mother's distress. She may have also been denying her feelings and reactions toward her new stepfather. I felt she didn't understand (or didn't wish to admit) the harmful influence of her boyfriend, and maybe others as well, who allegedly persuaded or intimidated her into using illicit drugs.

Our discussion will focus first on the issue of substance use and abuse and its ramifications. We will then turn our attention to the interpersonal aspects of Lisa's case as they relate to her boyfriend and her other friends. Judaism has much to say about both matters.

THE JEWISH RESPONSE

According to Jewish law, there are three reasons why Lisa must not use illegal drugs and mind-altering substances. First, the body is sacred and actually belongs to God, and, therefore, it must be treated with great care. Any habits or practices that have an adverse effect on the body and health are forbidden in Judaism. Accordingly, since illegal or illicit drugs have potentially harmful effects on health, their use is prohibited by Jewish law. Additionally, the use of mind-altering substances is prohibited because of the potentially harmful behavior that may result, injuring not only oneself, but others as well. In this regard, we speak not only of illicit drugs, but also of related activities such as driving under the influence of alcohol or controlled substances. Causing physical harm to others is strictly forbidden in Judaism.

Finally, the law of the land is the law by which Jews must abide, as long as those laws do not directly contradict Jewish law, against worshiping idols or causing harm to others, for instance (Gittin,10b). Underage drinking and the use of illegal substances are against the law in this country, and Jews are compelled to obey these laws.

So how does Lisa begin the process of rectifying her dangerous and harmful habits? How do we get her to return to living a life in which she is not harming herself and others, a life in which the consequences of all her activities assume primary importance in her mind? In Judaism, the key word is "return" or in Hebrew, *teshuvah*. Jews understand this term to mean "returning" to the way in which God wants us to act. Returning, that is, to a time of purity—purity of the body and purity of actions.

Jews don't believe in the concept of original sin—that each of us is born a sinner. Instead, sinful and improper behavior is a choice, and that choice is subject to change. It's interesting to note that one of the Hebrew words for "youth" is *bachur*. The infinitive connected to the root of this word is *livchor* meaning "to choose." Adolescence is certainly a time of much choosing. One makes choices ranging from what one is interested in academically to the extracurricular activities toward which one is drawn. Adolescents choose their peer groups and the careers that might be interesting to pursue. Developmentally, however, adolescents seem particularly unable to connect the choices they make with the consequences of these choices on their lives. Their unique perception of their own invincibility, while of course erroneous, is often cited as an explanation for much of their high-risk behavior.

The change we strive for when we regret our actions or the choices we have made is a "return" to a time when we were free of this behavior. This process involves only (yet substantially) two steps: a change of heart and a change in action. In biblical times repentance, or teshuvah, required sacrificial rituals at the Temple. Along with other prophets however, Micah tells us to shun sacrifices and suggests to us the correct action:

> Shall I approach God with burnt offerings,
> Would the Lord be pleased with thousands of rams,
> Shall I give my first-born for my transgression?
> He has told you, O man, what is good, and what is required of you . . .
> Only to do justice and "to do goodness" (to love acting mercifully)
> And to walk modestly with your God.
> (Micah 6:7–8)

The Three Steps of Repentance

There are three steps in the process of teshuvah. The first and perhaps the most difficult is recognizing the behavior in question as sinful, or as in Lisa's case, harmful to herself and to others.

The second step is asking for forgiveness. This requires courage and empathy—traits that many of us do not have. Seeking forgiveness certainly doesn't always come easily, but it is an essential step in the process of "return." In Judaism, we learn that we must ask for forgiveness directly from those against whom we have sinned before we can approach God to forgive us for those sins.

The third and final step in the process of teshuvah is making a commitment to change. Realizing that one has done wrong does little good if the harmful actions are repeated.

Using teachings and concepts from two programs and incorporating the concept of teshuvah, we can devise a plan for Lisa and help her chart a new path for her life.

Drug Abuse Resistance Education

The first program is DARE—Drug Abuse Resistance Education. In this program teachers and law enforcement officers target students with curricula that change with each grade level. If done effectively, it introduces young people to the social, medical, and legal problems of drug use. DARE's goals in the high school program include:

1. Getting students to act in their own self-interest when facing high-risk, low-gain choices.

2. Teaching students how to resist peer pressure and other influences in making their personal choices.

Alcoholics Anonymous

The second program from which we draw is Alcoholics Anonymous (AA). AA has a twelve-step program to help alcoholics beat their habits. The twelve-step program includes:

1. Taking a moral inventory of one's self—a fact-finding and fact-facing process to understand and deal with the causes and conditions of one's life.

2. Making a list of all persons who have been harmed as a result of one's alcoholism. The alcoholic must then be willing to make amends to those people.

Entering this program, a participant receives a number of promises, among them that feelings of self-pity and uselessness will disappear and that her whole attitude and outlook on life will change.

Lessons for Lisa and for Us

How does this apply to Lisa? We mentioned that the recognition of one's own sins and shortcomings is the first step in teshuvah.

Lisa must understand that her behavior is harming herself and others, which essentially is the same as the first step in the AA program. Furthermore, Lisa must acknowledge the wrong that she has committed in the form of wounds and damage to herself and also in terms of harm done to others. The anguish she is causing her mother is the prime example. This may require a number of sessions in order to break through Lisa's denial of her problem. It may also require some education in the form of demonstrating to her the devastating effects drug use has had on other teens.

There are now striking photos of blood flow to the brain as well as brain scans showing that people who use drugs have altered activity within the brain itself. These and other educational tools could be used in an attempt to teach Lisa the harmful effects of drug use. Joint sessions with her mother and a professional counselor might also help to correct Lisa's misconception that her drug use is "no big deal." This first step is the toughest, requiring persistent effort and trying the patience of healthcare providers, counselors, and Lisa's loved ones.

The second step in teshuvah is similar to the second step in the Alcoholics Anonymous program: Lisa must be honest and open with those who have been hurt by her actions. This especially refers to her mother. She must apologize to those harmed physically or emotionally by her behavior.

One of the prayers that Jews recite during *Yom Kippur* (Day of Atonement)—as we mentioned, the holiest day of the year for Jews—is a confessional prayer or *vidduy*. We ask God for forgiveness for, among other things, lying and other impure speech, breach of trust, practicing deceitful behavior, and wronging our neighbor. On this most holy day, Jews read from the book of Jonah in which God sent Jonah to Nineveh to announce its imminent destruction because of its residents' sinful behavior.

The residents repented and changed their way of living, and "God saw what they did, how they were turning back from their evil ways. And God renounced the punishment He had planned to bring upon them, and did not carry it out" (Jonah 3:10). This is a powerful lesson for Jews, made more so by the fact that it is read on such a holy day. The path to full recovery and forgiveness is thus quite clear.

In Judaism, the recitation of this confessional prayer is a necessary step in repentance. Saying we are sorry brings harmful actions to light and lays them bare. This step is difficult for most of us and may be embarrassing as well, especially because it involves seeking forgiveness directly from those harmed. However, only by taking this step can one demonstrate a full recognition of the harm one has caused others.

The third step in Lisa's teshuvah would begin with the two steps of the DARE program as described above: acting in her ultimate self-interest and revisiting and neutralizing the influences that brought her to this point. No matter what Lisa wishes for her future, the use of illicit drugs will not help her achieve it. Whether she wants to become an athlete, an entrepreneur, a social worker, a teacher, a parent, or any combination of these or other choices, she will be poorly served by using drugs. She may want to have close friends, a family and a stable home life, but she will instead likely find herself isolated and without close relationships. She may also find herself with a criminal record, will probably be unhealthy, and will risk losing the love and support of those dearest to her. Lisa's final step in teshuvah is to resolve to change her behavior when faced again with temptations and negative influences.

Lisa might protest that this program is too tough and that she doesn't have the capacity to achieve it. Jewish teaching begs to differ. In his Mishneh Torah (commentary on the Torah),

Maimonides teaches us, "Do not imagine here what the foolish say, that God decrees that every one from conception shall be righteous or wicked. Each individual may become wise or foolish, merciful or cruel, and similarly with all other attributes. There is no one to compel or draw a person to one path or another. He himself inclines to the path which he chooses" (Maimonides, Mishneh Torah, Treatise 5, Ch.5).

Maimonides also teaches us that the only way we know if we have achieved proper teshuvah is if, when we are faced with the same situation in which we initially chose poorly, we are now able to make a better decision.

One of the first steps that Lisa needs to take is to stop surrounding herself with others who have unhealthy, undesirable, and illegal habits. After all, "He who walks with wise men shall be wise, but a companion of fools shall be destroyed" (Proverbs 13:20). All of this—the entire program—is within Lisa's grasp and ability. The choice of all that we do, whether good or bad, is in our hands. We are reminded of the oft-quoted verse that Jews read in Deuteronomy which says, "I have set before you life and death, blessing and curse; therefore choose life" (Deuteronomy 30:19).

Dealing with Peer Pressure and Preserving Our Boundaries

Having dealt with the issue of substance abuse, we now turn to the second issue, the interpersonal aspects of the case that caused, or at least enabled, Lisa's situation to come about. Specifically, Lisa's plight involves possibly coercive behavior from her boyfriend and perhaps some of her other friends. Resisting this coercion will require courage on Lisa's part.

The Bible has a number of stories in which otherwise ordinary women show extraordinary courage. For example, the daughters of Tzlofhad petitioned Moses for the property of their deceased father, which otherwise would have gone to the clan as a whole, since there were no surviving sons, and daughters were not allowed to inherit property. We read that God supported their claim and directed Moses to transfer Tzlofhad's inheritance to his daughters (Numbers 26:33; 27:1–11).

The Bible also tells of Egyptian handmaidens who, against the explicit instructions of the Pharaoh to kill Israelite male children, performed perhaps the first-ever act of civil disobedience by refusing to practice this infanticide. Instead, they fabricated a story about how hardy the Israelite women were, claiming that they gave birth before the midwives even arrived. One of the infants saved was, of course, Moses (Exodus 1:15–17).

In her book *Sarah Laughed*, Vanessa Ochs teaches lessons from the stories of biblical women. One of the stories she relates involves the origins of the Jewish holiday of Purim in which an anti-Semite, Haman, has the tables turned on him by the king. At the behest of the king's Jewish wife Esther, Haman is put to death. Esther had kept her Jewish heritage a secret until its disclosure became necessary for her to help save the Jewish people.

The story that is of interest to us here doesn't involve Queen Esther. It concerns the queen who preceded Esther and who was dethroned by the king as punishment for her disobedience, Queen Vashti. Ochs adapts the story in her book:

> For one hundred eighty days, Ahasuerus, King of Shushan, displayed the vast riches of his kingdom and the splendor of his majesty for all the men of Shushan to behold. At the end of this period, he held a banquet in the court of his palace garden. Royal wine in ornate golden beakers was served in abundance, as befits a king. The palace stewards were ordered to keep the wine flowing. "There will be no limits!" the king declared.

At the very same time, Queen Vashti, the wife of King Ahasuerus, held her own splendid banquet elsewhere in the palace for the women.

On the seventh day of the king's feasting and drinking, when the king was utterly drunk, King Ahasuerus ordered his seven eunuchs to bring Queen Vashti before him wearing her royal crown so he could display her beauty to the people and the officials. For she was a beautiful woman.But Queen Vashti refused to come at the king's command.

The king burned with fury. He consulted his sages learned in procedures and asked them, 'What shall be done, according to law, to Queen Vashti for failing to obey my command?' They advised him, 'If it please Your Majesty, issue a royal edict that Vashti shall never enter the presence of King Ahasuerus.' In this way, other women would be cautioned to obey their husbands. (Ochs, 165)

Vashti knew what would be in store for her had she gone. She would be forced to strip naked and dance for the drunken hordes. Her dignity would be stripped away as well. "No," she said, "I will not go. I refuse." As a result, Vashti was banished from the king's presence. She may have lost her throne, but Vashti retained her full measure of dignity.

This is a story with a lesson about one's self-image and dignity. It is also a story about creating boundaries that must be respected, involving not only drug use, but other activities as well. In our contemporary society, there seems to be a correlation between a whole host of abuse-related and behavioral issues: date violence, substance abuse, sexual promiscuity and eating disorders to name but a few (Silverman, J.G. et al., *Journal of the*

American Medical Association 286[2006]:572). These behaviors tend to cluster in vulnerable individuals. While a correlation between one behavioral trait and others doesn't prove cause-and-effect, there appear to be behavioral patterns that place some young people in at-risk categories. Although the remedies and treatments for such individuals are complex, the Bible is replete with examples of figures who overcame personal tribulations and great odds to perform subsequently in a heroic way.

Lisa must realize that her life is significant and valuable. After all, she certainly has talents and gifts that can be shared with others, bringing self-fulfillment while making others happy. Lisa needs to keep in full view that which is most important to her and the goals towards which she strives. In this regard, she needs to realize that she has caused pain to someone close and dear to her—her mother. Lisa has caused damage to her own health, and she has set herself on a course to alter her future drastically and unfavorably. Lisa needs to be somewhat "selfish," viewing her actions and interactions in the context of what is best for her. We all have problems and issues in our lives, but like the rest of us, Lisa has the capacity to deal with them constructively and to overcome them. She must not give in to the urge to conform, but rather she needs to pursue her own aspirations and dreams.

APPLYING JEWISH TEACHING

Acknowledge and respect the sanctity of each individual. This includes your own emotional and physical well-being as well as that of others.

When you have compromised this sanctity, follow the three steps of repentance: admitting to yourself the improper behavior you have performed, sincerely apologizing to those affected, and resolving to change your behavior so as not to repeat these actions.

Be selfish—make decisions regarding your own behavior that are in your enlightened self-interest, creating boundaries that protect your physical and emotional health that must not be violated.

PART THREE

COPING AS WE FACE THE END OF LIFE:
OURS AND OTHERS'

Chapter 9

A LOVED ONE IS SUDDENLY GONE.
HOW DO WE GO ON?

Agnes's Case: *"Since Frank died, nothing matters anymore."*

Even before entering the examination room, I knew this would be a difficult visit. Agnes's husband of more than fifty years had died several months earlier. I had sent her a condolence note, but today's visit was Agnes's first to the office since his death. As soon as I entered the room, Agnes began to cry.

The Cause of Agnes's Symptoms

Agnes and I had known each other since the early 1990s. She was on medication for high blood pressure and had a rhythm disturbance of the heart known as atrial fibrillation. The upper chambers of the heart—the atria—are accessory pumps through which blood passes on its way to the ventricles. The ventricles then pump blood out of the heart and to the rest of the body. Normally, the atria not only serve as conduits for blood to pass through, but they also contract rhythmically, enhancing the amount of blood that the heart pumps.

In atrial fibrillation, the rhythmic contractions are replaced by a chaotic motion, still allowing blood to pass through, but no longer serving the function of an accessory pump. In most instances, patients don't miss the atria's contribution to the amount of blood pumped by the heart, but many do notice the irregularity of the atria's electrical activity. They frequently describe a "fluttering" of the heart, almost as though a butterfly was beating its wings inside the chest.

Medication can rather easily control this feeling. However, in times of stress, the adrenal glands pump extra adrenaline into the circulation, and the irregularity becomes more noticeable, causing discomfort to the patient. Agnes came to the office on this day complaining of an increase in her usually infrequent palpitations (a frequently uncomfortable awareness of the heartbeat). Given her emotional state, her physical condition was no surprise.

My examination indeed revealed that she was still in atrial fibrillation and that her heart status had not fundamentally changed. As we chatted about the likely reason for her increased symptoms, she did not even address her cardiac problem. "Since Frank died, nothing matters anymore," Agnes said simply.

A petroleum engineer, Frank had been active in Rotary and a pillar in the community. As is so often the case, Agnes's life revolved around Frank. His agenda was her agenda. Additionally, Frank took care of so many important things at home—he paid the bills, handled the investments, and made the travel arrangements for visiting their children and for vacations. He had been in control of much that was important to them.

Frank had been semi-retired. He worked as a consultant at the time of his death and often accompanied Agnes to the office for her appointments. An energetic and tall man, he suffered a major stroke at the age of seventy-two and died several months before Agnes's visit. Agnes and Frank had three children—one an hour's drive away and the other two out of state. Their children were with Agnes following Frank's death, but now the children and all the well-wishers had gone. Agnes was left to pick up the pieces, and her loneliness was evident.

As always, Agnes was well-dressed. She was a large woman with a round, expressive face. On this day, though, she seemed to have little interest in living, much less discussing her cardiac condition. Prolonged or excessive grief often requires the use of antidepressants, but beyond the issue of whether to prescribe such medications, Agnes needed a reason to go on with her life. Her palpitations would be easy enough to treat, but they were the least of what we had to deal with during her office visit.

Ongoing Grief

Agnes was relatively young, in her early seventies. She was otherwise healthy and spoke of the activities she had been involved with before Frank's death: a book club, a weekly bridge game with friends, and her church's Social Action Committee. The heart condition for which I was treating her did not limit her physically, and she had no other serious medical conditions.

It was difficult to know exactly how Agnes was handling the grieving process, or what role (if any) her faith played. Clearly, however, she was still openly and actively grieving at the time of her visit to my office. Now, several months after the death of her husband, the admittedly difficult transition to a more normal routine must begin for Agnes. What lessons does Judaism hold for those who are recently widowed? Might those lessons help Agnes?

THE JEWISH RESPONSE

In the Jewish tradition, one formally grieves for the loss of a child, sibling, parent, or spouse with rituals that are quite specific. There are very specific customs leading to and including the burial of the deceased. Following the funeral, there are two periods in the mourning process. A third mourning period is added when the deceased is a parent.

The traditions surrounding the funeral and the periods of mourning that follow aid the bereaved in the grieving process. One of our commandments is *halva'at hametim* (accompanying our dead to their final rest). This tradition requires a minimum of ten Jews comprising what is called a *minyan* (quorum), which then functions as the beginning of a support community. This commandment is not considered fulfilled until the grave is filled in, though many rabbis now only require that the casket itself be covered with dirt. The mourners themselves participate in this mitzvah, this commandment.

Getting Past Denial

Elisabeth Kubler-Ross and others have labeled the first stage of grieving as "denial." Essentially, they believe that the loss of a loved can be so shocking that we deny that it has really happened, or that it is final. We can't fathom such a terrible thing has occurred. The Jewish requirement to cover the casket of a loved one with dirt makes it very hard for denial to continue past this point. There is a very concrete recognition of the finality of death that occurs when one hears the sound of dirt and rocks striking a wooden casket.

Mourners in the Jewish tradition also either rend their clothes upon hearing the news of the loved one's passing, cut a piece of clothing at the funeral, or symbolically cut a ribbon that is then worn to symbolize the torn clothing. This custom began with

Jacob, who, upon hearing the (albeit false) news that his beloved Joseph had been killed "rent his clothes, put sackcloth on his loins, and observed mourning for his son many days" (Genesis 37:34). Such behavior symbolizes the tearing of the heart, and the torn ribbon or clothing is worn throughout the ensuing week. This phase is, of course, the most intense period of the mourning process.

Shiva (The First Seven Days of Mourning)

In Judaism, the first grieving period after the funeral is called shiva which lasts seven days and comes from the Hebrew word for the number seven. This week begins immediately following the interment of the body. It is a time for family and friends to visit and share the grief with those suffering the loss and is usually held at the home of the family whose loved one has died.

During the shiva period, mourners refrain from any type of work or celebration and are not supposed to be concerned in any way about their appearance. During regular prayer services, which are held in the home, mourners recite a prayer called the *kaddish*, a public sanctification of God's name. In fact, the kaddish prayer never mentions death. It is essentially an affirmation of faith and an acceptance of God's judgment. "The Lord has given, and the Lord has taken away; blessed be the name of the Lord" (Job 1:21).

In these first days of mourning the focus of the mourner is on grief, not on appearance or comfort. In addition from staying home from work, mourners cover mirrors, refrain from cutting hair and nails and from wearing jewelry and fragrances. Further, they neither clean laundry nor wear shoes, and it is traditional for mourners to experience physical discomfort by removing cushions from the chairs that they use. Often, mourners simply sit on the floor or on low stools; some even sleep on the floor. This period of mourning is so intense that even social graces such as the simple act of engaging visitors in conversation are simply not expected of the mourner during shiva.

In fact, visitors should not even greet mourners or initiate conversation; their presence is all that is expected. It is up to the mourner to decide whether to engage in conversation. Visitors do, however, traditionally bring food so that the mourners need not worry about even this most basic human need during this period of emotional upheaval. Many of the rituals during the first seven days come from the Book of Job. Job was a biblical figure whose faith in God survived the loss of his wealth and his health and the deaths of his children. During his mourning period, "Job's friends sat with him on the ground for seven days and seven nights. None spoke a word to him for they saw how very great was his suffering" (Job 2:13).

The purpose of this seven-day period is to absorb the loss of the loved one. During this time, Jews don't talk of "a better place" in which the deceased now resides. The time for adjusting to a now-changed life will come in due course. Instead, the focus is on pain and loss, allowing the family to feel the sting and hurt that the loss of a loved one brings about. "Today there is darkness" is one way a rabbi might begin a funeral service.

When the shiva period is over, mourners literally "get up" from their grief. At the conclusion of the morning service on the final day of shiva, it is traditional for several friends to escort the mourner on a walk in the neighborhood while other relatives and friends put the house back in order, uncovering mirrors and replacing cushions. This marks the end of the first period of mourning.

Sheloshim (The First Month of Mourning)

The next period of mourning is called sheloshim from the Hebrew word that means "thirty." This period of time stems from the length of time the Israelites mourned the death of the great prophet Moses (Deuteronomy 34:8). In fact, a similar tradition is carried on in the United States in which Americans fly their flag at half-staff for thirty days upon the death of a leader, such as a former president. Grieving is still encouraged but to an extent that is much less intense.

During sheloshim, mourners return to work and to normal living but continue some rituals of mourning. For example, they continue to say the memorial prayer at services, but at their local congregation rather than at home. Additionally, they are not to attend parties or other joyous events, particularly those in which music is involved. They continue of course to be comforted by loving friends and extended family. When a parent has died, this period of mourning is continued for an additional eleven months.

As one can see from this graded mourning process, the rabbis who derived this custom some two thousand years ago clearly understood human nature long before modern psychologists described the developmental stages of grief.

Memorializing Loved Ones

Beyond the grieving process described, Judaism has traditional ways of preserving the memory of loved ones who are deceased. For example, it is a Jewish custom to name a baby after a beloved relative who has died as a way of ensuring that the deceased person's memory is continued. There is also a tradition to conduct a brief ceremony unveiling the grave marker any time between the end of the sheloshim period and one calendar year after death. Each year after that, the children of the deceased remember their parent by lighting a candle that burns for twenty-four hours on the *yahrzeit*, or anniversary of the person's death.

It is also traditional for children to attend a prayer service and recite the memorial prayer on the anniversary of a parent's death. This traditional prayer is called the kaddish, the same prayer that is said during the shiva period mentioned above. In addition to a child's recitation of this prayer for a parent, kaddish is also said on the anniversary of the death of a child, sibling, or spouse.

Additionally, a special memorial service is added to regular holiday services in the synagogue four times a year. This memorial service is called *Yizkor* which is Hebrew for "He (God) will remember." These four occasions occur on the concluding day of the festivals of Passover, which celebrates the liberation of the Jews from slavery in Egypt; *Shavu'ot*, which commemorates the receiving of the Torah from God; *Sukkot*, during which we rejoice in God's bounty on earth and construct temporary dwellings that symbolically resemble those in which the Jews lived during their wandering in the desert; and *Yom Kippur*, the day on which Jews atone for sins committed during the prior year.

At any of these opportunities for remembering loved ones, it is traditional to donate to *tzedakah* (charity) and/or study religious texts in the name of the loved one being remembered. Our tradition holds that this is a way of helping to elevate the soul of the departed, ensuring its arrival or continued presence in the "world to come." (Although there is some ambiguity in rabbinic teachings regarding the exact meaning of "world to come," it generally refers to what becomes of the soul once the body has died.)

Agnes's Grief

Although we don't know Agnes's religious beliefs, specifically how they influence her process of mourning, it is clear she is still engulfed by grief. There is an old saying that "the long way is the short way," meaning some processes or journeys cannot be circumvented or shortened with respect to the mourning process. We may fool ourselves into thinking that short cuts exist. For instance, some may try to return to activities quickly, immersing themselves in work, study, or organizational meetings and functions. When we walk this path, however, and attempt to avoid the mourning process, we find that we only delay the grieving process. We spend much time going "backwards," eventually finding our way back to the normal grief response. Loved ones and medical care providers must respect the fact that recovering from the loss of a loved one takes much time and requires much support.

Agnes is currently in the early grieving process where "yearning" is the most salient emotion. A recent study delineating the stages of grief suggests that it is normal for this to go on for some time, but for many people, these raw emotions should begin to normalize after approximately six months (Maciejewski, P.K. et al., *Journal of the American Medical Association* 297[2007]:716). It is therefore too soon to conclude that Agnes needs additional treatment, such as medication, for her grief and loss. It is not too soon, however, for her support network to begin to try to lift her out of her emotional abyss.

Only after Agnes navigates her way through an appropriate and thorough grieving process will she be able to move on with her life effectively. In Judaism this is important because life is the most precious gift that we have. We learn from the biblical Abraham story that we are each taught to "make our lives a blessing" (Genesis 12:2). Agnes still needs to be a mother to her children, who are also grieving the loss of their father. She may also have grandchildren who will want to know what their grandfather was like and who will want to preserve his memory.

Making One's Life a Blessing

Agnes must strive to make her life a blessing, which will also reflect on Frank. Her loved ones need Agnes to show not only grief but also courage and the determination to enrich their lives with her presence and attitude. We read of King David's realization that little is to be gained from excessive grief and that, indeed, it may hasten physical demise:

> I called to You, O Lord;
> To my Lord I made appeal,
> What is to be gained from my death,
> Can dust praise You?
> You turned my lament into dancing,
> You undid my sackcloth. (Psalms 31:9–12)

As Agnes's emotions evolve, her family may benefit from some interesting findings that have been discovered in Jewish social research. One conclusion is that the death of a parent is often an impetus for returning to being active in one's congregation or house of worship. An additional, and perhaps surprising, finding is that surviving spouses, children, and grandchildren often incorporate some of the traditions of the deceased into their own lives. In Judaism, this might be demonstrated by leading the family *seder* (ritual meal) at Passover or making a favorite *mitzvah* (good deed) of the deceased one's own. This might involve donating to a specific charity or supporting a particular program at a school or house of worship.

Now Agnes can honor Frank by making his memory a blessing. How would he want her to act? Wouldn't he want her to take care of herself and to find enjoyment in her life? Wouldn't he want her to be a shining example of courage and a source of love for her children and grandchildren? Wouldn't he be proud of her work in her church's Social Action Committee? Frank's good works in the community need not end as a result of his death. With the love and continual support of family and friends, now Agnes can make certain that these good works do, in fact, continue. Indeed, she may be able to comfort herself while honoring Frank's memory by carrying on an activity that had been important to him during his life. Agnes has much to live for and accomplish—both in spite of Frank's death and because of it.

In Judaism, the answer to death is life.

APPLYING JEWISH TEACHING

When a loved one dies, do not attempt to avoid grief and the full grieving process. But when grief is excessive and prolonged, it can harm you physically and spiritually and can also be harmful to those with whom you come in contact.

Respond to death with life-affirming actions. The most sincere and productive way to honor the deceased is to enhance the lives of the living. This is done with specific actions that would make the deceased happy and proud.

Chapter 10

---◦◦◦◦---

LIFE SUPPORT:
WHEN AND WHEN NOT?

Phil's Case: *"He wouldn't want to go on this way."*

"Dr. Roffman, Phil can't breathe." Phil's wife was terrified. This story is one of two hospital admissions, a couple of years apart. Phil was a seventy-six-year-old man who had had a heart attack six years earlier but had recovered well and had no lasting disability. His heart function was diminished, but he had had no other major medical issues until he was diagnosed with myelodysplasia three years ago. Sometimes leading to leukemia, this is a condition in which the bone marrow becomes sluggish and contains abnormal cell forms. A patient with myelodysplasia often has impaired ability to fight infections. Until now, Phil suffered no ill effects from either his heart or bone marrow condition.

During an office visit last year, Phil had given me an advance directive—a written document stating a patient's wishes for his health care should terminal or catastrophic illness befall him. In the directive, he stated that he didn't want to be kept alive by "artificial means." This generally means that the patient rejects the use of a ventilator and other life support measures.

Critical Symptoms

His wife's call interrupted what had otherwise been a quiet weekend for me, but much was about to unfold. I told Phil's wife to call 9-1-1 immediately. When I assessed Phil in the emergency room later, he had fluid in the lungs, causing him to be short of breath. This was due to a condition known as congestive heart failure. Given Phil's heart condition, the symptom was not unusual, but why now? What had caused this condition to appear so suddenly? Phil was also found to have a fever, and his chest x-ray suggested the presence of pneumonia. In Phil's case, the pneumonia put a strain on his heart, which was not up to the challenge. Hence, fluid had begun to fill the lung spaces, resulting in a lack of oxygen in the bloodstream and subsequent shortness of breath.

Phil's mental status was impaired and his blood oxygen level was perilously low. If he was to survive, he would require a ventilator, an apparatus that would enable us to deliver more oxygen to his bloodstream. The ventilator would enable him to be sedated while the pneumonia and congestive heart failure were treated. What about the advance directive? Didn't that cover just such a situation? Wasn't the use of a ventilator just the sort of artificial means that Phil did not wish to be connected to in order to preserve his life?

Phil's Family. Should Aggressive Care Continue?

Phil wasn't alert enough to allow me to have an informed discussion with him about the alternatives at this point. His wife and children were at the hospital and, while discussions were cordial, there was clearly a difference of opinion among the family members. Phil's two children wanted his wishes as stated in his advance directive respected. After all, he had heart and blood disorders, and he was physically limited by other conditions—arthritis, visual impairment, etc. For the children, the issue was clear-cut: no ventilator, just "comfort measures," meaning that we should take steps only to relieve any pain or discomfort Phil might experience during his plight.

Phil's wife wasn't so sure. After all, there was a good chance that with antibiotics and diuretic therapy to dry out his lungs, Phil's health could be restored to what it had been before his current dire illness. It would not necessarily be an easy hospital course, but relief and improvement were certainly feasible.

What was the right thing to do? What would Phil want us to do if he were fully coherent? Would that have even mattered? After all, in the throes of congestive heart failure and pneumonia, would his judgment be sound? His advance directive was completed when he was rational and comfortable, but was this the "terminal" condition envisioned in the directive? In other words, was a potentially reversible condition what Phil had in mind when he signed his advance directive?

In 1996, the Israeli Knesset (Parliament) grappled with just such an issue in preparing rules concerning a patient's bill of rights. After consulting with religious, philosophical and legal scholars, legislators established that informed consent is unnecessary as long as the patient is in grave danger. They also argued that "there are reasonable grounds to suppose that, after receiving treatment, the patient will give his retroactive consent."

I felt that the proper course of action was to intubate Phil (that is, insert a tube into his windpipe), placing him on a ventilator to help him breathe. I explained to the family that while they were free to discharge me from Phil's case, I didn't feel that this was the situation that Phil envisioned when he wrote the Advance Directive, and thus, it should not be the final word. The family allowed me to proceed with my plans, and minutes later, Phil was indeed placed on a ventilator.

Phil's Recovery and Subsequent Deterioration

He was given medicine for his heart failure and was also given antibiotics for his pneumonia. After three days, Phil was able to breathe effectively on his own, enabling us to remove the ventilator. He was discharged from the hospital a week after his admission, and although it would be some time before Phil regained his strength, he eventually made a full recovery from his pneumonia and his bout of congestive heart failure. When I saw Phil in the office after his discharge, he was weak but clearly relieved to be over the worst of his acute illness. He expressed neither anger nor disagreement with my decision to treat his condition aggressively by intubating him and placing him on a respirator.

Over the next year and a half, Phil's physical condition remained relatively stable; he was able to enjoy his family and stay out of the hospital. He then suffered a stroke, and his myelodysplasia advanced—his blood count now suggested full-blown leukemia.

Shortly after this, I was asked to see Phil in the hospital where he had again been admitted with shortness of breath. Although he was not on a ventilator, he had been receiving antibiotics, blood transfusions, and breathing treatments to raise his blood oxygen level. Still, his breathlessness had become worse. Phil looked exhausted. His stroke prevented him from being able to communicate adequately, and he was barely coherent. Furthermore, his bone marrow was producing very few of the healthy white cells that could aid in fighting his infection, and his chest x-ray again showed that Phil was suffering from a combination of pneumonia and congestive heart failure.

Naturally, the issue of the ventilator arose once more. This time my recommendation was different. Now, his wife and his children were in accord. Phil was not intubated and was not placed on a ventilator. I gave Phil some additional sedation so that he might not suffer unnecessarily, and he died the following night with his family at his bedside.

Was this situation sufficiently different from Phil's first episode of congestive heart failure and pneumonia to warrant such a fundamentally and fatefully different course?

THE JEWISH RESPONSE

The role of the physician in the final stages of a patient's life has been the subject of much discussion in Judaism. Much of this discussion has centered on cases and situations just like Phil's.

Life Is Sacred

The practice of active euthanasia (the hastening of death by, for instance, the administration of life-ending medications to a patient who is suffering from a terminal illness) is contrary to Judaic teachings. Similarly, assisted suicide is not allowed under Judaic law. On March 12, 1997, the Conservative movement's Committee on Jewish Law and Standards published a summary statement on this subject. They concluded that in light of the Jewish view that life is sacred and that God has infused humans with life in His image, only God can decide when life is to end. Although we as loved ones and caregivers must strive to relieve pain and emotional suffering to the extent possible, suicide and the assisting in suicide is a violation of Jewish law. No one can take one's own life, assist in another's effort to end his or her life, or ask others to assist in the effort to end one's own life. Does this statement apply to Phil? As we shall see, the situation Phil faced was different and called for a different response.

Although Phil's death was allowed to ensue without exhausting every possible medical intervention, the decision was fraught with emotion. Judaism struggles mightily with this issue. Judaism is most definitely a life-oriented faith. Death is treated as a most unwelcome inevitability. One generally hears little in synagogues regarding what becomes of one's soul after the body has died. In fact, even the Bible emphasizes this life-centered orientation as opposed to death.

> What is to be gained from my death,
> from my descent into the Pit?
> Can dust praise You?
> Can it declare Your faithfulness?
> (Psalms 30:10)

> The heavens belong to the Lord,
> But the earth He gave over to man.
> The dead cannot praise the Lord,
> Nor any who go down into silence.
> (Psalms 115:16–17)

Relating to Phil's case and contrary to active euthanasia, Judaism condones passive euthanasia (for instance, the removal of life-preserving machines) under specific circumstances. Is there a major difference between the Jewish approach to this issue and a more secular viewpoint?

In a purely secular system of laws and customs, we may assign much importance to both personal autonomy and individual freedom. In the American tradition, each person has the right to decide how to care for his or her own body and health. Of course, even in such a system, the well-being of others must be taken into account. For instance, may a person choose to decline treatment for tuberculosis? What happens when he rides in a subway where his cough may infect others? Just such a case was in the news recently, where a man with active tuberculosis was apprehended after traveling on an airplane. He was subsequently forced into treatment, lest he infect others (CNN, July 13, 2007). So even within a secular framework, the rights and wishes of others must be considered regarding some medical choices. As a general rule, though, autonomy reigns in America.

Within a religious framework, though, the "Other" to be considered is God. Judaism teaches that our bodies and our lives do not truly belong to us—they belong to God. Only God may decide when one's life is over. Further, Judaism teaches that humans were created in God's image. At a time and in a place where human sacrifice, infanticide, and human killing for sport were common and accepted practices, the following was written: "And thus God created the human being in His image. In the image of God, He created the human being; male and female, He created them" (Genesis 1:27). If humans were created in God's image, then every person has a spark of the divine within. Each person is of infinite worth. A Talmudic teaching states that, "He who saves one life, it is as though he has saved an entire world" (Mishna Sanhedrin 4:5). Far from treating life as a disposable entity, we spare no effort to save a life. Then from God's perspective, we are compelled to view medical choices.

Additionally, Judaism believes not only in the infinite value of each life, but also in the infinite value of each moment in that life. These are the reasons why suicide and assisted suicide are strictly forbidden in Judaism.

Judaism regards each person as an entire universe. The sanctity of human life is of paramount importance. It follows that enhancement of health and preservation of life is commanded of us. Indeed, the preservation of life is of such importance that it takes precedence over almost all other commandments. The only exceptions to this—the only commandments that must never be disobeyed—are the prohibitions against murder, adultery and idolatry (Sanhedrin 74a). Thus, when an elderly patient of mine became ill on the Sabbath a couple of years ago, her Orthodox rabbi pleaded with her to seek medical care even though this would involve such activities as riding in a vehicle—an otherwise forbidden activity on this sacred day.

An additional point to establish in our discussion is that decisions regarding limiting (or even withdrawing) medical care are relevant only to those with serious and chronic illnesses. It does not, for example, pertain to the person involved in a serious automobile accident or to the patient who becomes gravely ill from an infection following surgery. In those situations, Judaism mandates that all possible measures that would restore health be employed. This was the case when Phil was initially seen in the hospital. Yes, he required "artificial means" in the form of a ventilator to keep him alive. At the time, there was sufficient reason to believe that he would be able to survive this event and would be able to breathe on his own once again.

Rejection of the Hastening of Death

In their books, Rabbis J. David Bleich (*Bioethical Dilemmas*) and Elliot Dorff (*Matters of Life and Death*) fully discuss the issues of care for the terminally ill. In its strictest and most observant form, Judaism rejects the hastening of death no matter how sick the patient. It regards treatment in even the sickest of patients as required by Jewish law. Indeed, the notion of even writing an advance directive, in which the patient expresses his or her wishes with respect to medical care in the event of mental incapacity, is moot. Any and all measures must be used at all times.

This view suggests that drugs, medical devices, and procedures were all endowed to us by God, to be used in order to preserve life. Medical care is an extension of divine help. There is thus no distinction between "ordinary" and "extraordinary" in the treatment of the gravely ill.

The only exception in these cases exists when the patient is certain to die within seventy-two hours. But there is a problem here. Does the seventy-two-hour rule refer to Talmudic times, before intravenous medicine and the use of ventilators and pacemakers allowed us to keep even the sickest person "alive" for many days or even weeks? Can anyone be so prescient as to know who fits into this category? It would seem that since we can virtually never be certain that a gravely ill person will die within seventy-two hours, maximum medical therapy is required in all cases.

Is this the conclusion of all Jewish teaching? Although aggressive treatment for all seriously ill patients is the standard in Judaism, does Judaism ever allow medical providers to let nature take its course? Is it ever acceptable to withhold treatment? Is our obligation to attempt to prolong life in whatever form absolute and inviolable? As Jewish teachings will show us, there is indeed some room for discretion.

Treatment of the Critically Ill

Readings and discussions in the Talmud (Avodah Zarah 27b) allow us to conclude that in a moribund person whose death is imminent, there is no obligation to perform actions that will simply delay actual death. This person is called a goses (a flickering candle). Active intervention by medical personnel on behalf of the terminally ill is not mandated. There is a Talmudic story about a great rabbi, Yehuda HaNasi, who was gravely ill and certainly near death. He was suffering greatly, yet his disciples continued to pray for his life to be prolonged. His maidservant realized how great his suffering was and how hopeless his situation was. She wondered, "Were the disciples' prayers all that stood between the Rabbi and death?" She intentionally dropped a jar, and when it broke, the attention of the Rabbi's disciples was temporarily distracted. At that very instant, the Rabbi died. Significantly, the maidservant was neither chastised nor punished for her actions (Ketubot 104a).

There seems to be general agreement in Judaism that once a patient becomes a goses, medical treatment may come to a halt, as such treatment is merely a hindrance of the natural process of death. And although it may not always be clear as to when this condition is met, most would recognize when a moribund person with a terminal condition has entered into just such a state. The decision to be made is whether one's interventions are actually prolonging life or merely delaying an early death. This situation applied to Phil during his second hospital stay. Further aggressive treatment, including the use of a ventilator might have delayed death for a time, but it would not have extended Phil's life in any meaningful way.

A "Terminal Illness" May Not Mean a "Terminal Patient"

The circumstances are different, however, when discussing someone with a "terminal" illness, for whom active intervention might prolong life for months or even years. Such was the case when Phil was first examined in the hospital with shortness of breath a year and a half previously. A person in this condition is a *terefah* (an imperiled life). The withholding of treatment is not allowed in such patients (Dorff, 200). For example, in an otherwise alert patient who has widespread cancer, the diagnosis of pneumonia would mandate treatment.

Because no one has a crystal ball, we cannot be certain how much additional life aggressive treatment would add. In almost all instances though, it is clear when dying patients are in their final throes. In those uncommon instances when such clarity isn't apparent, aggressive care is warranted. All measures are employed in the preservation of life.

These principles apply also to the withdrawal of treatment, such as removing a patient from a ventilator or discontinuing intravenous medicine, such as antibiotics. If there is any realistic hope for recovery, such treatments are to be continued. On the other hand, in those cases in which death is most certainly imminent, it is felt that withholding or withdrawing supportive measures merely removes impediments to dying and is thus allowed.

This "staged" approach of Judaism with respect to care for the critically ill mirrors its concept of death itself (Dorff, 232). (Indeed, this approach is also apparent in the nuanced Jewish views on the beginning of life, as they pertain to the argument roiling our country about abortion. For a discussion of this issue, see Gordis, *Does the World Need the Jews?*) As life nears its end, different standards of care may be required. On one hand, a patient may have an incurable but manageable illness, but now be afflicted with another, curable condition. For this person, Judaism mandates fully aggressive care. On the other hand stands the person whose condition is akin to a "flickering candle," one who is truly and unquestionably in the final stages of life. For this patient, comfort measures are sufficient.

Our Treatment of Phil

This was our guiding principle in treating Phil. When he first arrived at the hospital with congestive heart failure and pneumonia, he was known to have a serious blood disorder. However, treatment of the acute condition enabled him to live meaningfully for more than an additional year. By any interpretation of Jewish law, this treatment was appropriate. However, when he became mortally ill the following year with leukemia, reduced mental capacity from a stroke, and again pneumonia and heart failure, the medical response was different.

Sometimes, the line is indistinct. If there is any doubt, we must err on the side of keeping the patient alive, and all means necessary ought to be taken to preserve and maintain life. However, once it is clear that medical efforts will certainly be futile, the process of dying should be allowed to proceed. The side of the line on which the patient is placed is usually quite clear. Phil was clearly on the "other side of the line" during his final admission to the hospital and was allowed to die in a dignified way, out of pain, and with his family at his side.

APPLYING JEWISH TEACHING

Given the sanctity with which Judaism regards human life, it is not up to us to decide when someone's life, even our own, may come to an end. All illness must be aggressively treated, though sometimes that aggressive treatment might mean only supportive measures and providing comfort.

If we are absolutely certain that death is imminent, medical treatment may come to a halt.

Chapter 11

⟨⟨⟨⟨⟩⟩⟩⟩

FACING THE STARK REALITY THAT OUR DAYS ARE LIMITED

Al's Case: *"The cancer doctor gave me three months to two years to live."*

The difference in Al's appearance was difficult to bear; I had taken care of his heart condition for several years, and he had lost fifteen pounds since I last saw him six months earlier. He had had a heart attack ten years ago and required coronary bypass surgery. Al had done well since, experiencing virtually no chest pain and controlling his high blood pressure. His heart seemed to be stable with no indication of angina or heart failure.

The Medical Circumstances

The news this time involved a different organ and was far worse. Al had some problems with swallowing several months ago and an endoscopy was performed. This procedure uses a small tube with a tiny camera at the end to examine the digestive tract.

Al's test revealed the presence of cancer within the esophagus—the conduit connecting the mouth and the stomach.

The diagnosis of cancer certainly doesn't carry the same sentence of early death as it did a generation ago. Many advances in therapy have occurred. Chemotherapy, radiation techniques, immunotherapy, and surgery have all increased the expected chances of survival in patients with the majority of malignancies. Nonetheless, what has not changed is that once cancer is far along, it usually results in rather early death. To make matters worse, some cancers are especially virulent, hiding from detection while they invade other organs or spread into unreachable areas.

This was the case with Al. Although he sought care promptly once his swallowing problems began, the cancer had already spread into surrounding structures and was not amenable to surgical removal. Also, esophageal cancer is not especially responsive to either radiation or chemotherapy. Thus, if surgical removal of the entire cancer is not possible, the outlook is especially grim. When Al had his surgery, the doctors could tell at once that some of the cancer was left in his body and that it would spread inexorably, resulting in death. There were still some treatment options, but while they might extend Al's life, they would not cure the cancer. "The cancer doctor gave me three months to two years to live," he said. His voice was quieter than usual, and his deep brown eyes seemed to search mine for an answer, as though his statement had been a question.

Al's Family

On this day, Al was accompanied by his wife of more than forty years. We had been through so much together. Al's brother, Lou, had moved to Dallas from New York twenty-five years earlier, following a heart attack that he was told would be disabling. With encouragement, medication, and a cardiac rehabilitation program, Lou was able to return to work. Because of additional coronary blockages that occurred during the ensuing years, he underwent a number of procedures on his coronary arteries involving tiny balloon-tipped catheters which inflated within the blockages to allow for additional blood to flow (a procedure known as angioplasty). All this care and treatment enabled him to live almost twenty additional years. Al had been supportive of his brother throughout, and when it came time for him to have his own coronary bypass surgery ten years ago, the closeness of the entire family was evident.

Al was the father of three and the grandfather of seven. Though he had retired from his job as a manufacturer's representative two years ago, he was constantly busy with volunteer work, with his family, and in particular with his wife.

Having recovered from his surgery, he had recently begun a combination of chemotherapy and radiation treatments while trying to cope with this devastating turn in his life. His hope now was that the cancer would respond to this therapy to at least some degree, extending his life. The oncologists didn't talk about curing the malignancy with this treatment, only slowing its growth. Al now sat before me, pale and somewhat gaunt. We both knew that this might be his last visit to my office.

THE JEWISH RESPONSE

Revisiting Moses

Does Judaism provide any guidance for how to act in such dire circumstances? One of the most famous figures of the Hebrew Bible, Moses, also faced imminent death, though it was decreed by God rather than being due to a fatal illness. As we recall from an earlier chapter, Moses and Aaron finally lost their composure during one of the many times that the Israelites complained about their circumstances in the wilderness (Numbers 20:1–13). Instead of speaking to a rock, causing it to supply water to the thirsty Israelites, Moses struck the rock. The water still spewed out, but Moses and Aaron were told by God that for not following His instructions, they would not live to lead His people across the Jordan River and into the Promised Land. Aaron's death, in fact, is first recorded just fourteen verses later. It is quite possible that Moses realized that his death was similarly soon to come. Later, God is much more direct and tells Moses, "The time is drawing near for you to die" (Deuteronomy 31:14).

Although the severity of the punishment has been a continual subject of discussion, our focus here will instead center on how Moses handled the edict. Moses's death takes place in Chapter 34. He is told of his imminent death three chapters earlier. We have no way of knowing for sure exactly how much time elapses within those three chapters of Deuteronomy. If we read the chapters, we see that Moses doesn't waste his time by complaining, becoming despondent, or trying to change God's mind. Indeed, he speaks to the entire congregation of Israelites, articulating some of the most beautiful and poetic passages of the Torah—words that include praise of the God who is about to take his life. He also manages to bestow to his people, referred to by God as "stiff-necked," a blessing (Deuteronomy, Ch. 33). Moses loved his fellow Israelites, though at times they drew his fury. Challenging Moses repeatedly during the years of their desert sojourn, Moses's followers still loved him deeply and would mourn him for thirty days.

Perhaps that is the origin of the Jewish expression *zichrono/zichronah livrachah* (may his/her memory be a blessing). When people in our religion pass on, we add this simple phrase after their name in the hope that they will be remembered for the good they did in their lives and for the blessings they gave to others during their time here on earth. We should all attempt to become a blessing to those who remember us. Moses remains a role model for us today, not only in his words and deeds during numerous trying circumstances as the Israelites traveled in the wilderness, but in the length of his life as well. According to scripture, Moses was 120 years old when he died. Our Jewish tradition today is to wish someone they should live to be 120, basically meaning that they should live a good long life, as Moses did.

Importance of a Good Name

Our tradition also teaches us the importance of a good name. "Rabbi Shimon taught: 'There are three crowns: The crown of Torah, the crown of the Priesthood, and the crown of God's Kingship. But the crown of a good name surpasses them all'" (Pirkei Avot 4:17). We are instructed to live our lives in accord with God's commandments so that we can merit such a good name. If we accomplish this, when we face the end of our lives, we will likely be allowed entry into the "world to come." No matter how long we live, life is but a brief moment in the great sweep of time. We would all like to live longer, but many would agree that quality of life is more important than quantity. We must use all our days wisely and cherish each moment.

Some Well-Known Battles with Cancer

There has recently been a spate of stories in the news media involving well-known people and their battles with cancer. These include the wife of Senator John Edwards, Elizabeth Edwards; *Newsweek* writer Jonathan Alter; politician and actor Fred Thompson; Presidential Press Secretary Tony Snow; and the former head of the National Institutes of Health, Doctor Bernadine Healy. Some of these figures have related firsthand stories and have given interviews that are emotionally compelling. They also give insights into how they have coped with such illness and the ensuing emotional upheaval.

As Elizabeth Edwards pointed out in a CNN interview with Larry King on April 12, 2007, we all face death. That's the ultimate fate for everyone. We are given only a finite number of days on earth. How we choose to spend them is up to us. Each day must thus be spent wisely, for we can't know when our days will be at an end. "There is no authority over the day of death" (Ecclesiastes 8:8). A life's worth cannot be judged by the number of its days but rather by what we have done with the days given to us and by what we leave behind.

In addition to using our days to the fullest, we must all strive to live in such a way that we have no major regrets. In a Talmudic story, Rabbi Eliezer teaches us to "Repent one day before your death." His disciples asked him, "But does a person know what day she is going to die?" The Rabbi answers the question. Because we do not know the precise day on which we will die, "All the more reason, therefore, to repent today, lest one die tomorrow" (Shabbat 153a).

In the interview with Larry King on CNN, Dr. Healy related advice given her by Jonathan Alter, the *Newsweek* reporter. Do not say that a particular cancer (or any other condition, for that matter) is incurable. What we should really say is that "It's not curable at the present time." There have been great strides in medicine. As stated by his doctors, the range of time that my patient Al might live reflects an uncertainty as to how he will respond to his medication and radiation. No one knows how a specific patient may respond to treatment. Given this uncertainty, there is always room for optimism and reason to continue to fight the illness.

We discussed earlier how cardiac patients who are depressed have a less favorable medical prognosis than those with a healthy mental outlook. A study that corroborates this finding beyond heart disease concludes that an optimistic attitude toward life is correlated with improved longevity (Giltay, E.J et al., *Archives of General Psychiatry* 166[2004]:1126). Certainly, correlation doesn't necessarily mean cause and effect. The studies that have shown this correlation do not include people with advanced cancer. Nevertheless, the data is worth noting. If nothing else, a positive attitude will surely make Al more pleasant to be with and will certainly enable him to be a shining example to his family of how to exhibit grace and spirit in the face of extreme adversity.

Looking Beyond Oneself

Even in illness, Al must try to be mindful and aware of those around him and of the searing memories that his illness will create for his family. Difficult though it may be, he must continue to be an example of courage and warmth for them. I am reminded of the funeral of Vice President Hubert Humphrey in 1978. Humphrey died after a courageous battle with cancer. Before becoming Vice President, Humphrey was the senior senator from Minnesota. He was a mentor for Walter Mondale, a man who would follow a similar career path—a senator from Minnesota who became Vice President. Mr. Mondale eulogized Hubert Humphrey by recounting his enormous zest for life, his commitment to helping the disadvantaged, and his valor and good nature as he battled his cancer. "Hubert taught us how to live," Mondale said. "And in the end, Hubert taught us how to die."

The closeness Al has had with his family certainly points to the many blessings that he has enjoyed. But what will he do now with the limited time he has left? As we have seen, Judaism teaches that he must continue to live, making the most of each day. Beyond the issue of how we spend the days we are granted in life though, one issue we will all face is what to do with our bodies and our organs when our time of passing comes.

Organ Donation

The issue of organ donation from the deceased brings out a possible conflict in Judaism. On the one hand, the human body is inviolable even in death. It must not be desecrated, and it must be buried promptly (Deuteronomy 21:22–23). Indeed, the human body is so sacred that it must not be left unattended from the time of death to the time of burial (Mishnah Sanhedrin 6:5). Even in death, the body is treated with the utmost dignity and respect. (This practice has led some of the Jewish faith to refuse to allow autopsies and even organ donations after death.)

Indeed, the Jewish tradition places such importance on the body that God has lent us that we are required to bury any parts that don't make it with us to the end of our lives (digits, extremities, and so forth.). Thus, when a suicide bombing causes the death of Jews, body parts are gathered for proper burial. The only exception to burial rite is when organs are donated to save or improve another's life.

These conditions notwithstanding, there is no greater commandment than the saving and preservation of life. The Talmud discusses the implications of what this obligation means, concluding that all commandments except the prohibition of murder, idolatry, or adultery (Talmud Yoma 82a) must be subservient to the saving of life. In this regard, all available resources must be used (Sanhedrin 73a, 74a) in the setting of a medical emergency in order to save a life. When this is no longer possible, attention should be turned to possible organ donation as a means to save the life of another.

Even beyond the saving of a life, the preservation of the body is so important in Judaism that, before allowing for the donation of, for instance, a heart or even a cornea, some in the Orthodox movement would require the identification of a specific person who would receive the organ—one whose life is in jeopardy or whose eyesight has been lost or is in peril. However, most rabbis would accept that given the modernization of medicine and the efficiency of organ banks, a proper recipient will be found. They would thus allow for the donation of corneas or other organs even before a specific recipient is identified.

Al may or may not be a candidate for organ donation, but for him and his family, this act may give additional meaning to his life. And what a wonderful way for his memory to be honored. Currently tens of thousands of patients await transplants because of poorly functioning hearts, kidneys, and other organs. Is there a more concrete way to save a life than to donate an organ? Information for patients regarding organ donation was recently published by the editors of the *Journal of the American Medical Association* (286[2001]:124).

The "Ethical Will"

There is also a tradition in Judaism of writing what is called an "ethical will." Here a person leaves a letter or discourse on the values that were important to him or her throughout a lifetime. These can include personal thoughts and reflections and can be drafted for any number of people who are important in one's life. Going all the way back to Genesis, we read in Chapter 49 of how Jacob gave his last thoughts to each of his sons. Later, Moses delivers farewell blessings to the people in Chapter 33 of Deuteronomy. In fact, some might argue that the entire book of Deuteronomy is a farewell message to the Israelite people. Still later, King David shared his desires for his son Solomon (Kings 2:1–12).

So we see that the Hebrew Bible has numerous examples of early ethical wills, as do the Apocrypha (sources that were not included in the final compilation of the Hebrew Bible). Later, we find examples in the Talmud. As the tradition continued, there are some famous examples of ethical wills from the Middle Ages, many of which can be found in *Hebrew Ethical Wills* edited by Israel Abrahams and published by the Jewish Publication Society.

The ethical will is again gaining popularity, and it is something Al may want to consider leaving for his family.

Don't Lose Hope

The history of the Jewish people is replete with innumerable persecutions and expulsions, including the most horrific—the Nazi Holocaust of the twentieth century. If there is one thing the Jewish people have learned from our storied past, it is that we must never lose hope. No matter what our predicament, we always held onto hope. And when our dream came true of reclaiming a homeland for the Jewish people after almost two thousand years of national homelessness, the song chosen to be the national anthem for the newly created State of Israel in 1948 was Hatikvah, which simply means, "The Hope." As a people and as individuals, this quality remains prominent in Jewish teaching.

So informed by the Jewish religion, what can we say to Al? Some of the possibilities are listed below. As we read over this list, isn't it striking that it could apply to all of us on any day of our lives? Why wait until we are facing imminent death? Certainly, there is something compelling about confronting our own mortality that makes us introspective and more open to change. There is no reason why we can't consider the components of this list at any time. Why wait? If not now, when? The hour may be later than we think.

APPLYING JEWISH TEACHING

Continue to do things that will make your life rewarding and fulfilling. To the extent possible, live each day as though you don't have a serious disease, while fighting your illness with a full cache of medical weapons.

Feel and display as much optimism and courage as you can muster. Continue to have hope but realize that you have much to do and not a day to waste. These traits will serve as shining examples to the loved ones you leave behind.

Remember that the memory of the righteous is a blessing. Be righteous in your behavior so that your memory will be a blessing to your friends and family.

Are there people with whom you need to communicate and reconcile differences? Any time would have been fine, but now is an especially good time.

If appropriate, consider giving the gift of one or more organs when the time comes. The events surrounding one's death are emotionally wrenching under the best and most expected of circumstances, so make your wishes regarding organ donation known to your doctors.

Write down your thoughts and reflections. These words will serve as a gift to those most dear to you. They will have an enduring and powerful impact.

PART FOUR

LESSONS LEARNED

Chapter 12

TEN COMMANDMENTS FOR COPING WITH ADVERSITY

On July 9, 2007, a feature on CNN reported on a study released by the Centers for Disease Control and Prevention (CDC). It showed that, as a class, antidepressants were the most commonly prescribed medications in America. While many of the patients taking these medications surely have clinical depression as defined in medical texts, the drugs have also been prescribed for simple situational sadness and anxiety. In the year analyzed by the CDC, 118 million prescriptions for antidepressants were filled. While there is much depression in our country, there is also much tension and unhappiness.

Changes in work environment, stressful family issues, and health concerns affect all of us at one time or another. As we said in the introduction, life has a way of confusing us, blessing us, and bruising us, sometimes all at the same time. How we cope with adversity, with the stones and arrows that life hurls our way, will ultimately help determine how happy and fulfilled we are. The data on antidepressant use in our country suggests that as a population we can do better.

We are blessed when we can observe and appreciate people who show grace and strength under duress. Forty-eight-year-old Sonia was in my office recently for an assessment of her heart function before beginning chemotherapy for breast cancer. While she was certainly sad about her plight, she was the embodiment of what we have discussed in this book. She had much to get well for, with a loving family and close friends, and she realized that the anticipated side effects from chemotherapy were simply what she had to go through in order to get well. She was as cheerful and optimistic as one could expect, and she was concerned about the well-being of her family as she endured what was certain to be a rough time ahead.

In another case, I could feel only sympathy for Wanda, seventy-four, who had been estranged from her widowed sister for many years. Her sister had become mortally ill with cancer, and in a magnanimous gesture, Wanda took her sister into her home for her sister's final days. Wanda came to me for an office visit some months after her sister died, and I couldn't resist asking her, "You had much time to spend with your sister during her final illness. What did you talk about?" "Missed opportunities," she said, choking back tears.

Are we also missing opportunities? Sometimes the greatest tragedies in our lives are not in the losses we suffer but in the potential blessings and joys we fail to realize. Wanda is like the rest of us. She is capable of acts of loving kindness, while at the same time, imperfect in her dealings with others. In fact, this is exactly how we find our biblical figures, from Abraham and Jacob to David and Solomon. The stories related to these figures show them to be very much like us—capable of kind and heroic acts, while fully capable of sinful behavior.

Maybe that is the reason why the lessons of the Bible are so compelling. We can relate to biblical figures in a very personal way. Like us, they are flawed. Many of the biblical lessons discussed in this book related to interpersonal actions. God, it seems, wants us to know that, while ritual is important, it serves mainly God. It is even more important to behave well to one another. On Yom Kippur, the holiest day of the Jewish year, observant Jews fast, refraining from eating and drinking from sundown to sundown. Indeed, we refrain not only from eating but also from any acts that would provide bodily comfort and pleasure, as we concentrate on how to serve God and each other better in the coming year. On this day, we read a portion of the Bible from Isaiah, Ch. 56 and 57:

> To be sure, they seek Me daily,
> They are eager for the nearness of God.
>
> Because on your fast day,
> You see to your business and oppress all your laborers;
> Because you fast in strife and contention,
> Your fasting today is not such
> As to make your voice heard on high.
>
> No, this is the fast I desire:
> To let the oppressed go free,
> It is to share your bread with the hungry,
> When you see the naked to clothe him,
> And not to ignore your own kin.

The emphasis on behavior toward others and on safeguarding one's health demonstrates that Judaism is a culture that emphasizes life. Preserving life, making the best of bad times while relishing and giving thanks for good times, and caring for ourselves and others are what matter most. We have seen les throughout the book of the importance Judaism places on health, relationships, and good deeds. If we internalize these lessons, the number of prescriptions for antidepressants will surely be reduced.

Inspired by the teachings of Judaism, we conclude with "Ten Commandments for Coping with Adversity."

1. ***Be grateful for all your blessings. Cherish and enjoy them.***

   To the extent possible, do not let illnesses or the occurrence of the inevitable and unfavorable circumstances of life interfere with joyful moments. Try to live each day as though you had no illness. Do your best to "compartmentalize" any adversities or illnesses you have, not letting them define you. Enjoy all there is to enjoy while recognizing the limited role that the acquisition of consumer goods plays in your lasting satisfaction with life. Take advantage of the health benefits of optimism.

2. ***Make your life relevant.***

   From a simple smile and kind word to the endowment of a charitable fund, all of what we do and say in our daily activities and contact with others has an effect. Make a difference. Look upon every interaction and task as an opportunity to leave a positive imprint on the world. It is never too late in your life to affect favorably your surroundings and heal a world that badly needs repair. Whether large or small, make a positive difference in the world.

3. *Greet people with a cheerful demeanor.*

   To a large degree, you can make each day "good" or "bad." Make each day as good as it can possibly be. Sprinkle smiles liberally. Cheerfulness will be returned to you by others and will help make every day as pleasant as it can be. When facing life's hardships, you will enjoy your days more if your interpersonal interactions are pleasant.

4. *Recognize that life is a precious gift.*

   Take proper care of your body, which is a gift from God. Be selfish about your physical well-being, your interests, and your safety—make decisions that will most likely help you attain and preserve optimal health. Do not let others adversely affect your decisions in this regard.

5. *Set aside time to appreciate family and friends.*

   Create and safeguard periods of time in which you can enjoy and celebrate your blessings. Set aside time also for rest and reflection. Do not skimp on the amount of time and attention devoted to these purposes, but rather regard these occasions as "holy."

6. *Don't rely on miracles for good things to happen.*

   Focus on the positives in your life and on what is possible. When you are ill, aggressively fight the illness as though it was your most important task. Face other hardships proactively by utilizing all the resources at your disposal. Make God's work your own, beginning with your own health.

7. ***Fulfill your family obligations but don't take on more than your share.***

    Teach your children to be independent and caring people who contribute to the betterment of the world. Respect, honor, and dignify your parents. Loving behavior toward your whole family will provide a good example to your children. Act in ways to ensure that you will have no regrets, but remember that you can do only so much. Don't be overburdened by your own limitations in these matters—you can control only so much.

8. ***Seek forgiveness, make amends, and repent.***

    Before you act or speak, replay in your mind what you are about to say and do. Pretend you have been given a chance to do or say it again. If you act sinfully in words or in deeds, repent fully and honestly. Interpersonal strife can affect your sense of well-being and even your health. Reconcile differences with those who mean much to you. If your life would be enriched by having a better relationship with a particular person, try to improve that relationship.

9. ***Do not excessively grieve the death of a loved one; do not excessively lament your own illness.***

    Certainly, grieve appropriately and fully for those who have died, but remember that ultimately, the best answer to death is life. The deceased are most meaningfully memorialized by performing good deeds in their honor and by acting in such a way that would make them proud and happy. We are in control of how we ultimately respond to all sorts of adversity—from the loss of a loved one to a setback in our own health.

10. ***Keep in mind how you want to be remembered.***
The memory of the righteous is a blessing. Be a blessing. Live ethically. Enjoy the things you do. Spread love and good cheer. No matter what your age and health status, prepare for your eventual death by writing an ethical will, considering organ donation, showing grace and courage in the face of illness and adversity, and most of all by expressing appreciation and love to those important to you.

Through countless lessons and embodied by numerous biblical figures, Judaism teaches us that whatever adversity we might encounter, the writing of our life's narrative is largely up to us.

SOURCES AND ADDITIONAL READING

Abrahams, Israel, ed. *Hebrew Ethical Wills*. Philadelphia: Jewish Publication Society, 1936.

Bialik, Hayim Nahman and Yehoshua Hana Ravnitzky. *The Book of Legends*. New York: Schocken Books, 1992.

Bleich, J. David. *Bioethical Dilemmas*. Hoboken, NJ: KTAV Publishing House, 1998.

Bolles, Richard N. *The Three Boxes of Life*. Berkeley: Ten Speed Press, 1978.

Cahill, Thomas. *The Gifts of the Jews*. New York: Nan A. Talese Doubleday, 1998.

Dorff, Elliot N. *Knowing God*. Northvale, New Jersey: Jason Aronson, Inc., 1996.

Dorff, Elliot N. *Matters of Life and Death*. Philadelphia: Jewish Publication Society, 1998.

Erickson, Eric. *Childhood and Society*. New York: W. W. Norton and Co., 1951.

Frankl, Victor E. *Man's Search for Meaning*. New York: Touchstone, 1984.

Gordis, Daniel. *Does the World Need the Jews?* New York: Scribner, 1997.

Gordis, Daniel. *God Was Not in the Fire*. New York: Scribner, 1995.

Hartman, David. *A Living Covenant*. Woodstock, Vermont: Jewish Lights Publishing, 1997.

Heschel, Abraham Joshua. *God in Search of Man*. New York: Farrar, Straus and Giroux, 1955, 1983.

Heschel, Abraham Joshua. *Man Is Not Alone*. New York: Farrar, Straus and Giroux, 1951, 1979.

Ochs, Vanessa L. *Sarah Laughed*. New York: McGraw Hill, 2005.

Sacks, Jonathan. *A Letter in the Scroll*. New York: The Free Press, 2000.

Sternberg, Esther M. *The Balance Within: The Science Connecting Health and Emotions*. New York: W.H. Freeman, Publisher, 2001.

Telushkin, Rabbi Joseph. *Jewish Wisdom*. New York: William Morrow and Company, Inc., 1994.

Wilson, Timothy D. *Strangers to Ourselves*. Cambridge, Massachusetts: The Belknap Press, 2002.

Zipes, Douglas V. et al., eds. *Braunwald's Heart Disease: A Textbook of Cardiovascular Medicine*. Philadelphia: Elsevier Saunders, 2005.

ABOUT THE AUTHORS

Dr. Joel Roffman is a cardiologist practicing in Richardson, Texas. He graduated from Boston University School of Medicine and after completing his post-graduate studies in Hartford, Connecticut, moved to Dallas, Texas, where he and his wife raised their family, and where he continues to practice.

In addition to maintaining a busy office practice, Dr. Roffman is chairperson of the charitable foundation for his sixty-eight physician group. He has taught Sunday school and high school science, coached youth sports for fourteen years, and is a past-president of the Southwest Region of the American Jewish Congress and the Richardson Chapter of the American Heart Association. He is currently a vice president of the Dallas Jewish Historical Society.

Rabbi Gordon Fuller is the congregational rabbi for Agudath Jacob in Waco, Texas. He holds degrees in Human Development from Northwestern University and in Social Work from the University of Chicago.

Rabbi Fuller was ordained as a rabbi in 2004. Prior to his current position, he served for twenty years in various Jewish educational leadership positions. In Waco, he has been particularly active in interfaith activities including serving on the Board of Caritas and the Greater Waco Interfaith Conference.